SOUTHWOLD
TO ALDEBURGH
THROUGH TIME
Michael Rouse

AMBERLEY PUBLISHING

Acknowledgements

My grateful thanks to Southwold photographer Stephen Wolfenden for his splendid photograph of the Jill Freud Company at Southwold. Stephen is the Company photographer and more of his photographs can be seen on the Summer Theatre website. He has also published two books of Southwold photographs: *To the Town* and *The Town Revisited, Portraits of Southwold*.

My main research sources are my own book *Coastal Resorts of East Anglia*, which was published by Terence Dalton in 1982. For that book I drew on many old travel books particularly Harry Brittain, *Rambles in East Anglia*, 1897; T. West Carnie, *In Quaint East Anglia*, 1899; C. S. Ward, *Thorough Guide to the Eastern Counties*, 1882. I have referred to *Southwold to Aldeburgh in Old Photographs*, compiled by Humphrey Phelps, Alan Sutton, 1991; used a Ward Lock guidebook from 1923/4 and searched various websites, including those of Southwold Museum, Dunwich Museum and Aldeburgh Museum.

My thanks to the manager and staff at the Cliff House Holiday Park for their help and allowing us access to go down to the beach.

I am grateful to Ben and his friend Annie, Lee, and Cassie and her friend Molly, for their company on some of the trips. All of my photographs were taken in September and early October 2011, with a few in February 2012.

Finally, my thanks to Sarah Parker, Joe Pettican, Lauren Newby and all at Amberley Publishing.

To the bravest of the brave – the lifeboat crews, past, present and future, not just on this part of Suffolk, but all around the coast of our island.

First published 2012

Amberley Publishing
The Hill, Stroud
Gloucestershire, GL5 4EP

www.amberley-books.com

Copyright © Michael Rouse, 2012

The right of Michael Rouse to be identified as the Author of this work has been asserted in accordance with the Copyrights, Designs and Patents Act 1988.

ISBN 978 1 4456 0772 6

British Library Cataloguing in Publication Data.
A catalogue record for this book is available from the British Library.

Typeset in 9.5pt on 12pt Celeste.
Typesetting by Amberley Publishing.
Printed in the UK.

Introduction

It is becoming a little joke with my children that when I set off from Ely to get to Southwold I arrive in Aldeburgh, and when I'm heading for Aldeburgh it is Southwold that I find. No matter, I love them both and rarely visit one without travelling along the coast to the other, through Thorpeness and Dunwich, and this book does the same.

The problem of accessibility may well explain why both small towns have retained so much of their charm and escaped some of the excesses of the holiday industry. Also, neither town had an entrepreneur with a 'grand vision' like Samuel Morton Peto at Lowestoft or Peter Bruff at Clacton.

This section of the Suffolk Heritage Coast is very much for those who love the sea, sand, shingle and fantastic fish and chips. 'Do you know what I like about Aldeburgh?' a father said to me, after he allowed me to photograph his two boys playing with model boats in the boating lake at Aldeburgh. 'There are no amusement arcades.' I understood all too well how expensive such arcades can be when you have children! Mind you, Southwold has a delightful pier with a small arcade, but it has no gambling machines, and there is also an irresistible and unusual amusement arcade that is genuinely entertaining. Southwold is also home to Adnams Ales, which is probably an attraction for some.

There was a time when there were concert parties on the pier. Elsie and Doris Waters, later to become the great radio favourites Gert and Daisy, made their concert party debut at Southwold in about 1924. For many years now Southwold has enjoyed Jill Freud and her company presenting their plays in St Edmund's Hall during the summer season; an entertainment that they also take to Aldeburgh. The world famous Aldeburgh Festival at Snape Maltings is also a highlight of the town's year. These cultural events are, I'm sure, enjoyed as much by the locals as by the visitors.

This book is all about holidays along this fascinating stretch of coast. The more obvious signs of the holiday industry are not so apparent, but for those who know it, this is a richly rewarding area with a fascinating heritage reflecting our relationship with that relentless North Sea. Much of the original town of Aldeburgh was lost to the sea. All within a few miles are the kingdom of Dunwich, where this once most important of towns surrendered itself to the sea, leading to the romantic notion of church bells still ringing under the waves, Slaughden, which has been lost to the sea, and Thorpeness, Glencairn Stuart Ogilvie's amazing early twentieth-century creation.

These small towns attract walkers, artists, writers and poets. George Crabbe (1754–1832) is the most famous son of Aldeburgh. Benjamin Britten, who lived with Peter Pears at the Red House along Golf Lane, now being renovated as the home of the Britten-Pears Foundation, took his inspiration for Peter Grimes from Crabbe's poem 'The Borough'. The stunning sculpture *The Scallop* by Maggi Hambling, erected on the beach between Aldeburgh and Thorpeness in November 2003, honours Britten and is pierced with a line from *Peter Grimes*: 'I hear those voices that will not be drowned'.

Woodbridge, born Edward Fitzgerald (1809–1883), is famous for his translation of the 'Rubiyat of Omar Khayyan'. He had a lifelong passion for the sea and wrote: 'There is no sea like the Aldeburgh sea, it speaks to me'. For me too, perhaps it is at Aldeburgh that the relationship between man and the sea is most strongly felt. Having said that, can there be a better tonic for the spirits than walking along the beautiful sea-washed sands of Southwold or exploring Thorpeness?

Welcome to a part of the Suffolk coast that has a very special charm all of its own.

Michael Rouse
Ely, February 2012

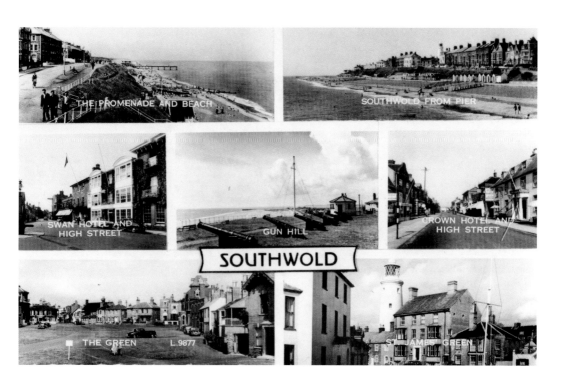

THE PROMENADE AND BEACH
SOUTHWOLD FROM PIER
SWAN HOTEL AND HIGH STREET
GUN HILL
CROWN HOTEL AND HIGH STREET
SOUTHWOLD
THE GREEN   L.9877
ST JAMES GREEN

Southwold, *c.* 1960

'We're having a very nice time here with lovely weather and very good food. We are staying at the Crown Hotel...' A card sent to Edinburgh from Southwold in 1960, just over fifty years ago, and Southwold is instantly recognisable except for the pier. It is this unchanging familiarity which makes Southwold so popular for retirement and holidays. C. S. Ward wrote in 1882, 'Southwold, without doubt, is the least obtrusive of all the East Coast watering-places that are accessible by rail.'

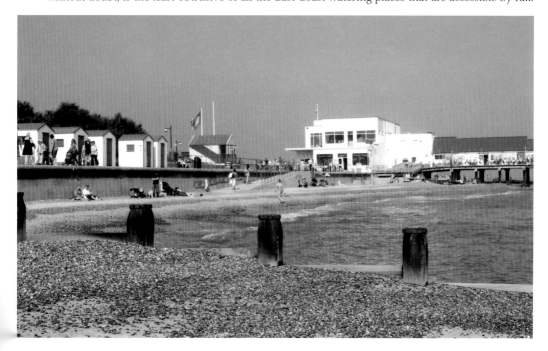

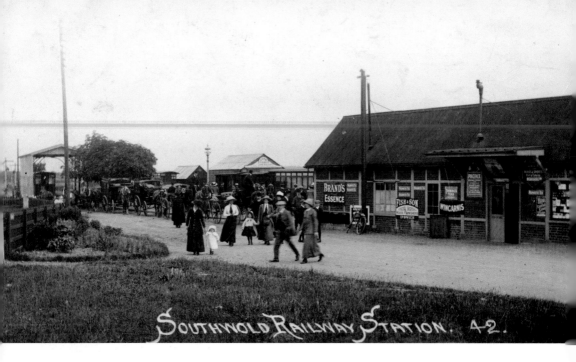

Southwold Railway Station. 42.

Southwold Railway Station

On 24 September 1879 an independent rail company opened a 3-foot gauge line to Southwold from Halesworth, 9 miles inland. As Ward wrote, 'the company issue an official timetable, but, luckily, on its outside page, they do not guarantee that the trains will keep to the times of starting or arriving as mentioned'. With its little blue locomotive and maroon coaches, it was the epitome of the 'crab and winkle' branch lines to the coast. The well known local comic illustrator, Reg Carter, (1886–1949) caricaturing himself by the sign, affectionately immortalised its eccentricities in two sets of postcards called 'The Sorrows of Southwold'.

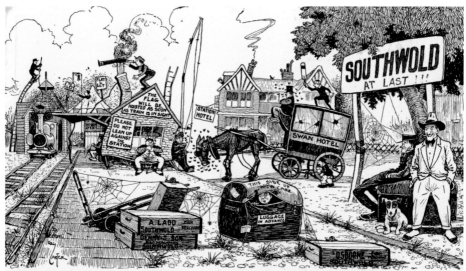

THE SOUTHWOLD RAILWAY – WAITING AT THE TERMINUS FOR THE DOWN EXPRESS WHICH IS SOMEWHAT LATE – A VERY UNUSUAL OCCURRENCE.

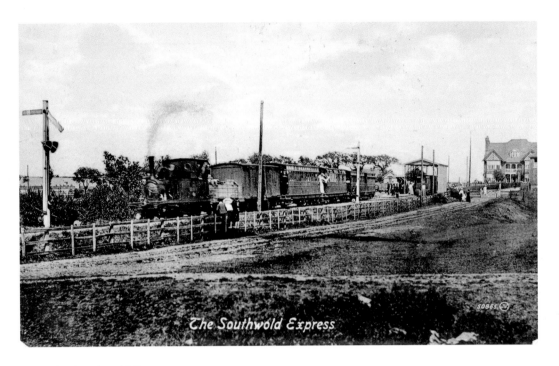

The Southwold Express

The Southwold Express

In the 1890s West Carnie described it as 'that quaintest of all toy railways'. The Board of Trade imposed a 16 mph speed restriction on the narrow gauge track and it was said it was possible to run and catch it up at Walberswick. It was a busy line, however; 104,197 passengers were carried in 1910 and 12,824 tons of freight conveyed. Coal and general merchandise were brought into Southwold, while milk, farm produce and fish were taken to connect with the main line. The line and the station closed on 11 April 1929 and much of the route is now a cycleway.

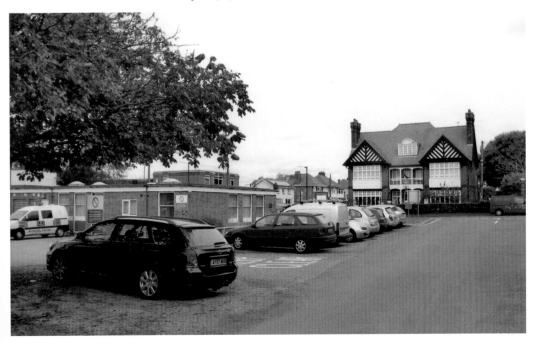

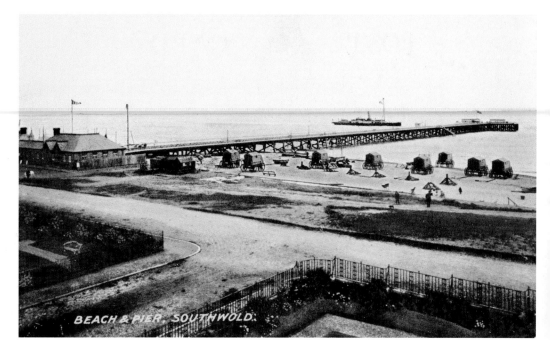

BEACH & PIER, SOUTHWOLD.

Beach and Pier Southwold

In 1900 the Coast Development Company opened an 800-foot pier as a landing stage for its Belle steamships. Despite the railway, in the early days, most holidaymakers arrived by sea. As car travel increased in the 1930s, Belle coaches began replacing the steamships. In 1934 the T-shaped landing stage was swept away in a violent storm. During the Second World War the army removed a section and it was struck by a mine in 1941. Despite repairs in 1948, in 1955 half of the pier was washed away in a storm and in 1979 another storm reduced it to just 60 feet in length.

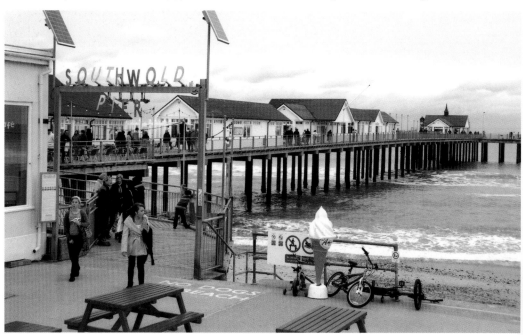

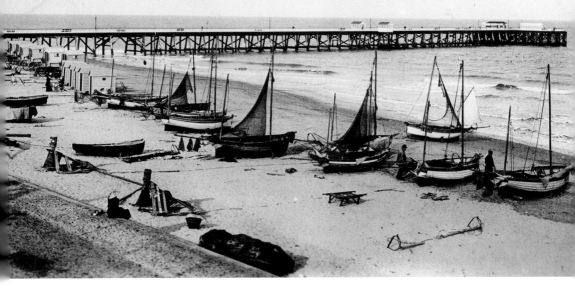

The Pier and Sands

The pier is now 623 feet long and not just a landing stage. Along its length are delightful cafés and shops, there is Tim Hunkin's water clock and his extraordinary machines in the Under the Pier Show. From the end of the pier, where the *Waverley* paddle steamer still calls every year, recreating its former history, there are wonderful views of the seafront and opportunities to fish. For those who want them there are sheltered places in the sun to sit and enjoy what has been voted the 'Best Tourism Experience in the six counties of East Anglia'.

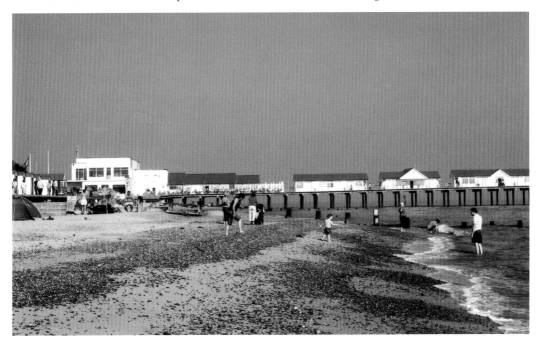

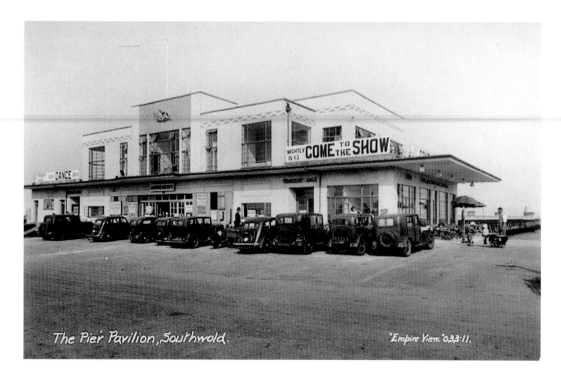

The Pier Pavilion, Southwold. "Empire View" 033 11.

The Pier Pavilion

In 1937 the original wooden buildings at the pier entrance were replaced by a two-storey pavilion with concert hall and amusement arcade. Today there are still small shops, an amusement arcade and a café. While the pavilion survived most of the damage to the pier, in 1987 what was left of the pier was bought for restoration. This was an act of love and great expenditure that was finally completed in 2001 when the pier re-opened. The following year it was deservedly named Pier of the Year.

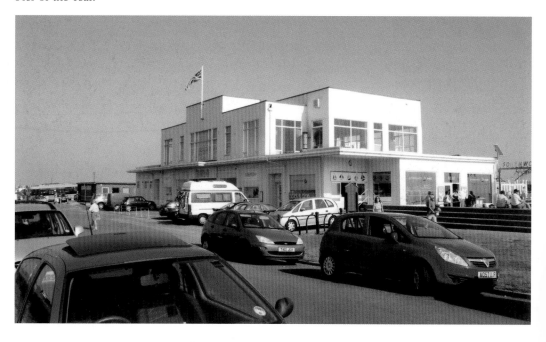

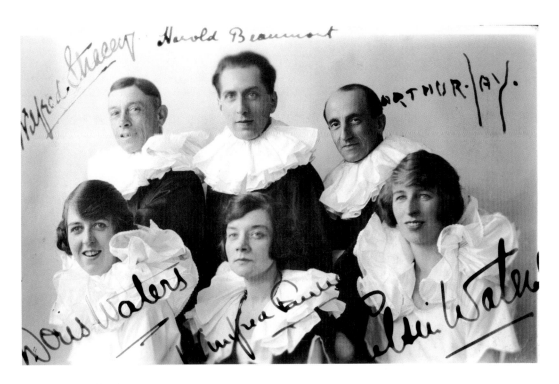

Concert Parties

Southwold had its concert parties and in around 1924 Elsie and Doris Waters were engaged for their first summer season as a piano and violin act. Later in the 1930s and '40s they became two of the biggest radio and recording stars, particularly with their Gert and Daisy routines. There are no concert parties today, but Jill Freud has been running her successful Summer Repertory Theatre at the St Edmunds Hall since 1984. Producing a varied programme each season, the company also performs in Aldeburgh. Below is the 2011 company. (Photograph by Stephen Wolfenden)

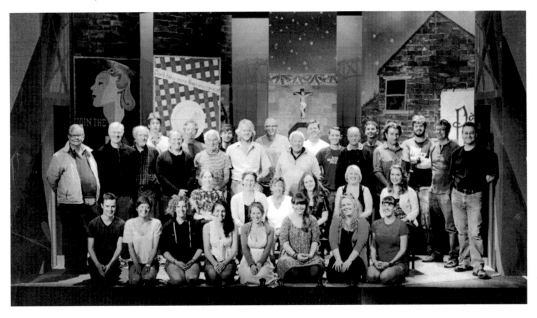

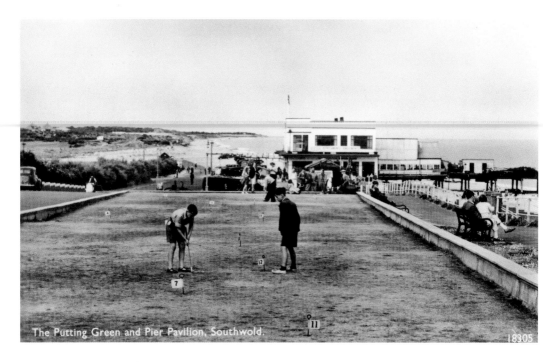

The Putting Green and Pier Pavilion, Southwold.

18305

The Putting Green and Pier Pavilion

This photograph looks like it was taken in the 1950s. The putting green is next to the promenade; now it is just across the road from the pier and close to the boating lake. A putting green is such a Southwold thing. Not for this resort the wild excesses of crazy golf but the more genteel seaside pursuit of putting.

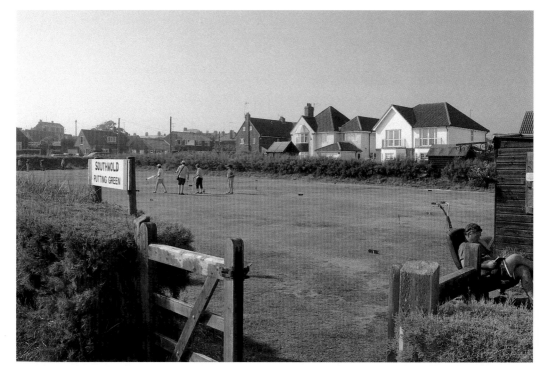

SOUTHWOLD PUTTING GREEN

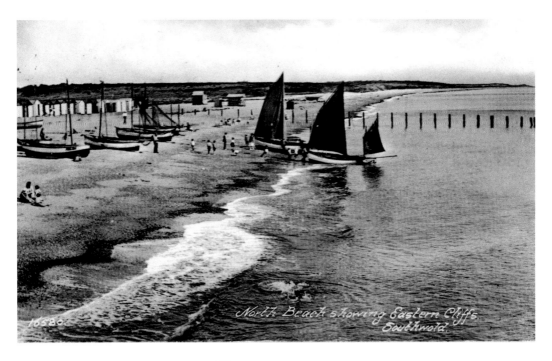

North Beach Showing Eastern Cliffs

In August 1932 the sender of this postcard was 'Delighted with Southwold' and remarks on the 'lovely bathing'. Today's view shows the boulder groynes and the sea wall, built in 1960, protecting the beach huts and the area behind, which is now a huge coach and car park in front of the boating lake and the marshes.

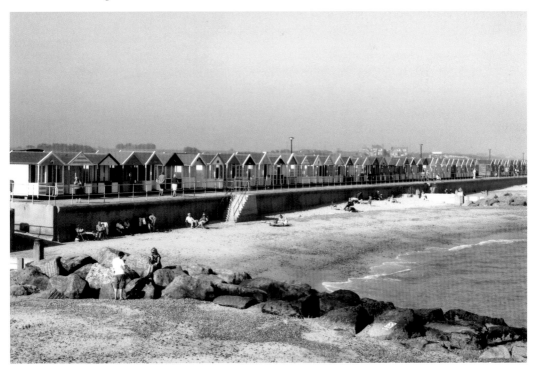

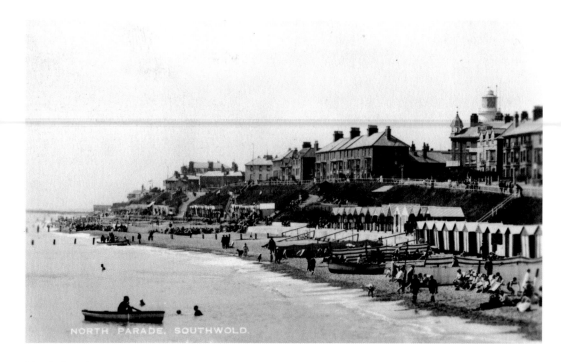

NORTH PARADE, SOUTHWOLD.

North Parade

In 1888 Harry Brittain took a steamer trip from Yarmouth to Southwold. The ship anchored off Southwold and they were ferried ashore in small boats. He remarked that the town 'has in the last few years sprung into some note as a watering-place.' He quoted Saville Clarke in *Punch*: 'Southwold's the place to get rid of dull care', but concluded 'dull care is not cast to the winds at Southwold in consequence of excessive gaiety, as, certainly, no duller town exists in East Anglia.' That is hard to imagine looking at this lively beach scene from between the wars.

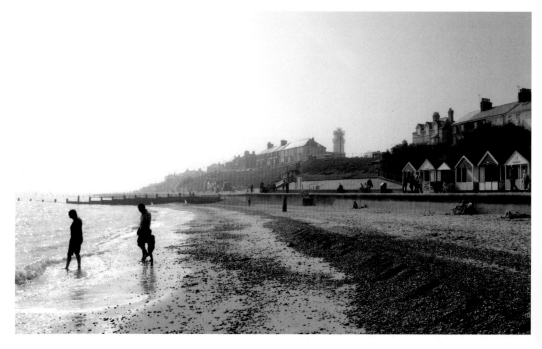

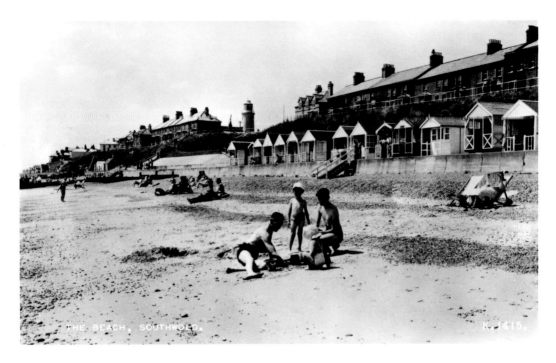

The Beach, Late 1950s

There is a timelessness about making sandcastles and paddling; doing so must be one of the secrets of a happy life. In the previous photograph, the luxury hotel the Marlborough can just be seen in the centre, above the terrace of houses. The Marlborough, which opened in 1900, was completely destroyed by enemy bombs on 15 May 1943. The name survives as a road name. It is impossible to miss it the skyline, as with the Grand seen in the next two photographs. In such an ageless seafront both buildings are missed.

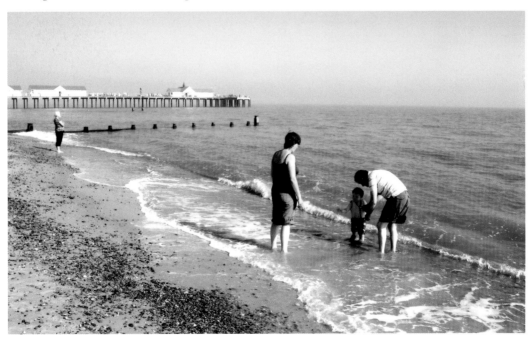

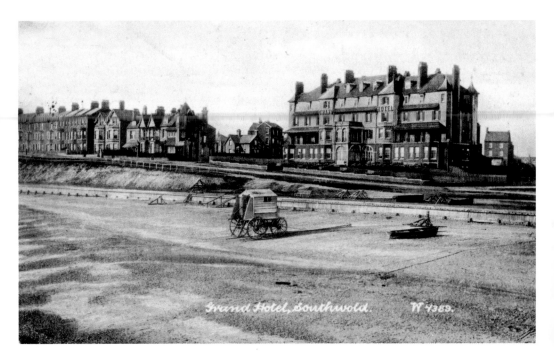

Grand Hotel, Southwold

Seen from the pier, the Grand was built by the Coast Development Company when they built the pier and laid out Pier Avenue. Opened in 1901, it was in a magnificent position, looking across to the full length of the pier and a short walk from the railway station where trains were also met by an omnibus. It boasted luxuriously furnished apartments, a spacious lounge, a lift, electric lights, and billiard, smoking and reading rooms. Like several hotels around the coast, it never recovered from being requisitioned for the army during the Second World War and was demolished in the 1950s.

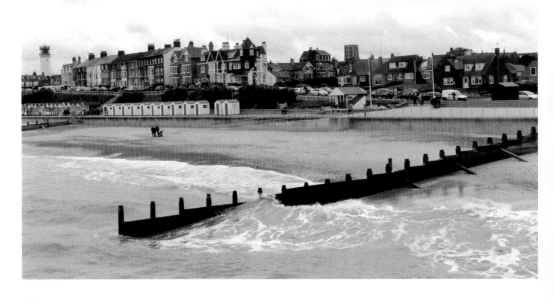

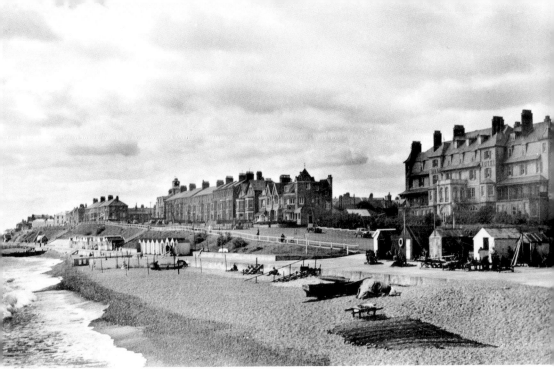

North Parade

It is the early 1950s and the Grand still stands. After Dunkirk, with the threat of German invasion, Southwold was seen as a frontline town. The beach was covered with barbed wire, mines were laid, trenches were dug and guns were installed to defend the town against attacks from the sea. Women, children and the elderly were evacuated and the town was closed to holidaymakers. Thirteen civilians were killed during bombing raids and many properties destroyed.

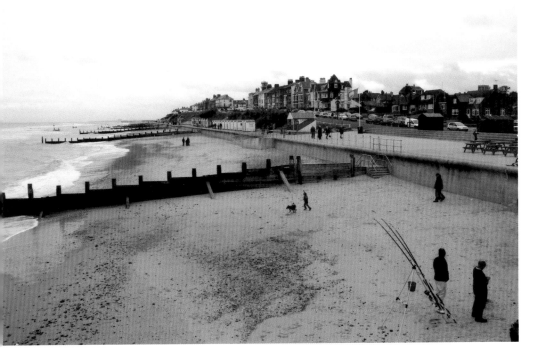

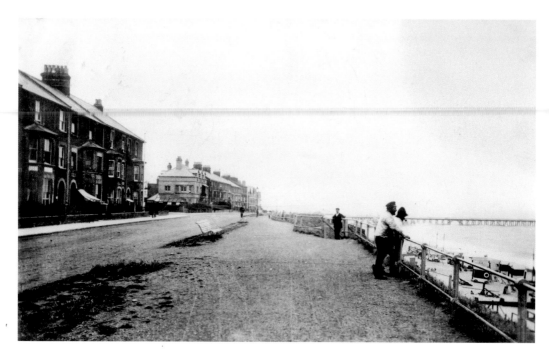

North Parade and East Cliff, *c.* 1913

It is August 1913 and Edie has sent her mother a card to say that she has just spent half a day in Southwold and is enjoying herself very much. Two fishermen lean on the rail and below them on the beach are bathing machines and fishing boats. In a year's time such a tranquil scene will be changed by the First World War. By the early 1930s, below, the bathing machines have gone and the deck chairs and wind breaks are neatly arranged for a relaxing holiday. There is an orderliness and gentility about the seafront.

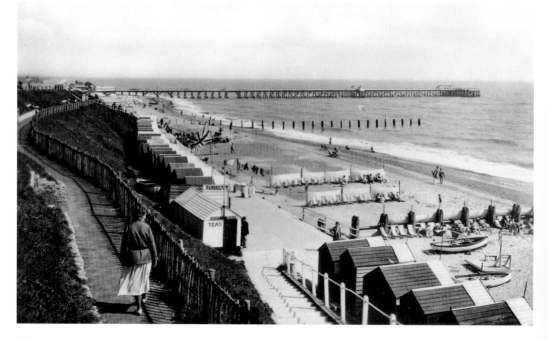

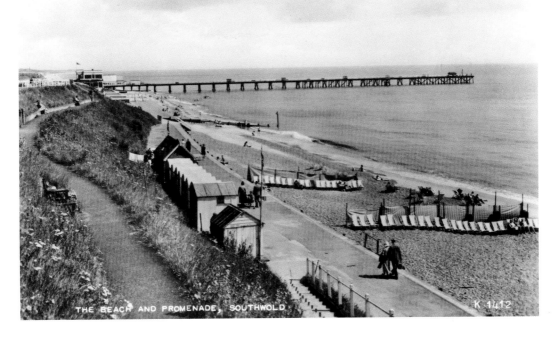

THE BEACH AND PROMENADE, SOUTHWOLD   K 1412

The Sands and Promenade

A new sea wall and promenade was completed between Gun Hill and Centre Cliff in 1950. It was then extended to the pier by 1955. This solid defence served the town well in the east coast floods of 1953, which though damaging the pier pavilion did not cause damage in the town. The deckchairs are still splendidly arranged south-facing in this 1950s photograph, ready for more customers to enjoy the sunshine and fresh air.

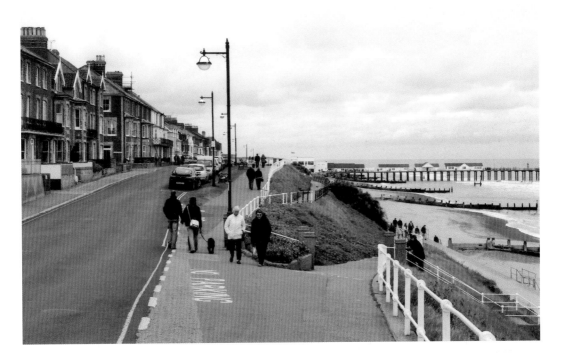

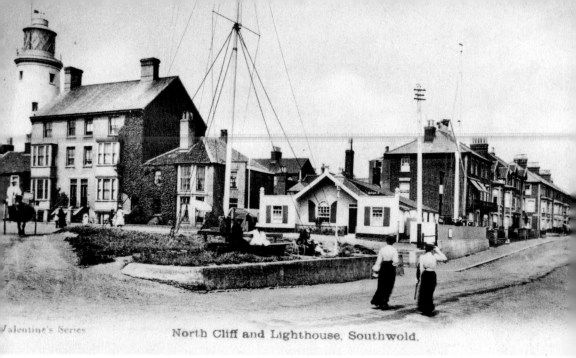

Valentine's Series   North Cliff and Lighthouse, Southwold.

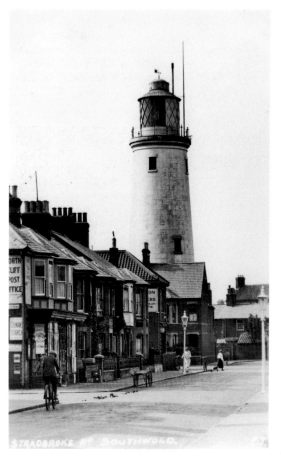

North Cliff and Lighthouse

As well as a pier, every seaside town should have a lighthouse! Southwold's was built by Trinity House in 1892 and rises over 100 feet above its cliff top situation. It was built beside the coastguard station. Some 1½ million half bricks were brought into Southwold on the railway and transported by local coal merchant Thomas Moy & Co. in a shuttle service of their wagons to the site. The main white light is visible for 18 nautical miles. In 1938 it was electrified and operated automatically.

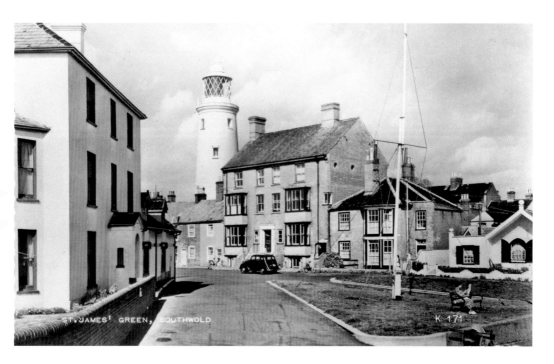

St James' Green

The flagpole used for signalling by the coastguard remains, but the coastguard is no longer there. The green seems to have changed little over the years. The two cannon that stand there today are eighteenth-century castings from shipwrecks in Sole Bay, which was where the dreadful sea battle between the British and French navies and the Dutch navy was fought in 1672, with terrible loss of life. The photograph from 1960 does show marked changes to the large house and a reduction in height, giving an even better view of the lighthouse.

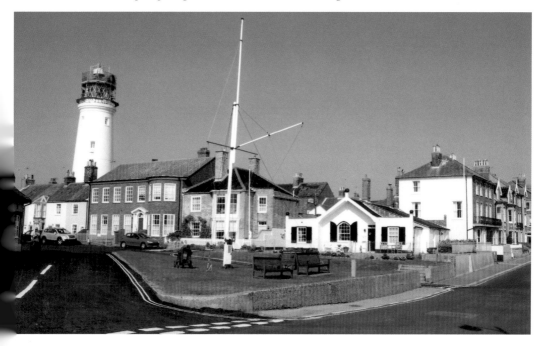

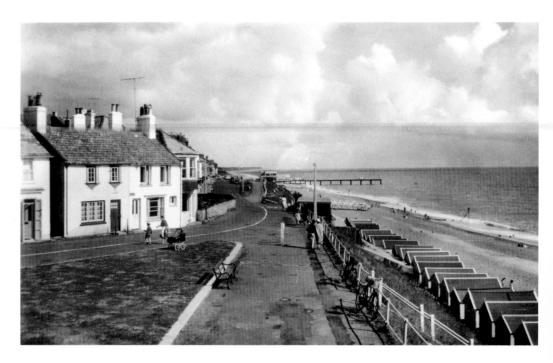

East Cliff Green

There are nine attractive greens, large and small, in Southwold. Some are attributed to the disastrous fire of 1659, designed to act as fire breaks. The small, triangular East Cliff Green provides fine views from its elevated position. This photograph, which appears to be from around 1960, shows the storm-damaged pier at about half its original length.

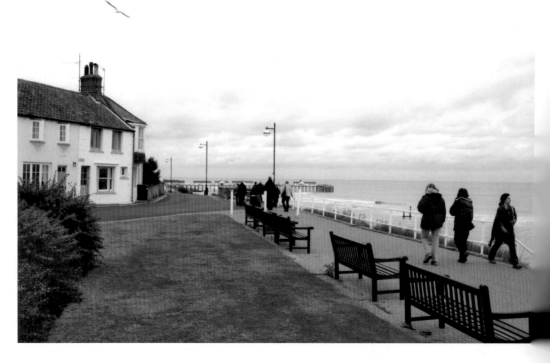

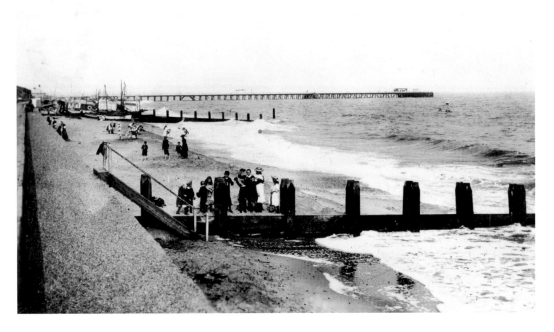

Sands and Pier

In September 1911 Harry sent a postcard to his teacher in Surrey in his best handwriting: 'I am having a nice holiday and hope to be back next Monday week, with love...' It is apparent that from a very early stage, as Southwold began to develop as a 'watering place', the authorities have been determined to protect its special character. In 1899, for example, bathing machine operators were asked not to permit bathing after 10 a.m. and Mr Thomas Davis was refused permission to have a candy stall on or near the beach.

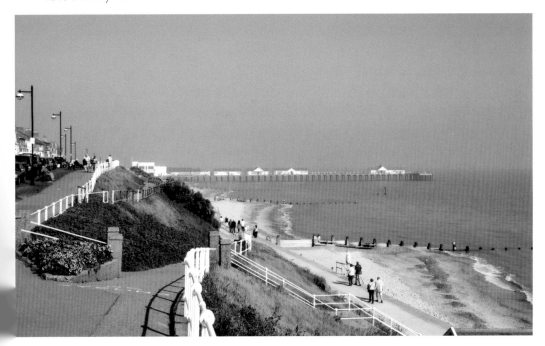

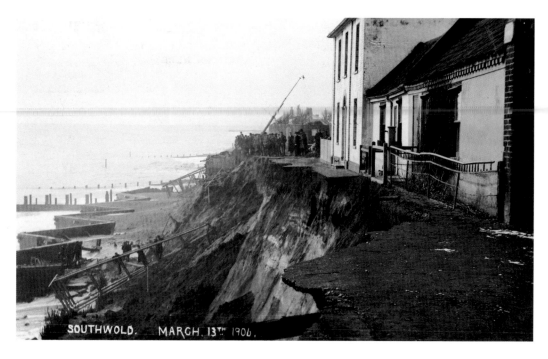

SOUTHWOLD. MARCH. 13TH 1906.

Damage Caused by High Tide, 1905

The Centre Cliff and nearby Sailors' Reading Room escaped this heavy cliff fall, as a result of which the cliff face was reinforced and defences were strengthened to prevent further damage. The Centre Cliff (seen below in about 1922) was not a hotel for very long. After the First World War it became the junior school for St Felix School, and after being requisitioned for military use during the Second World War it was converted into flats, minus its upper storey.

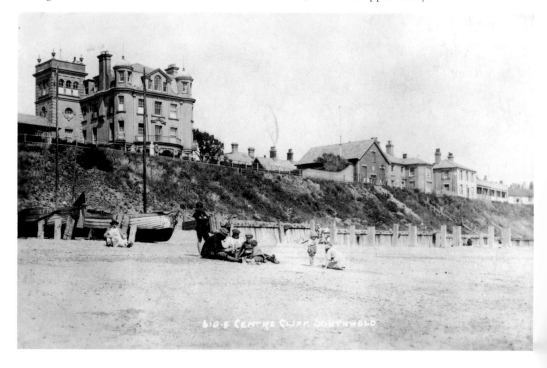

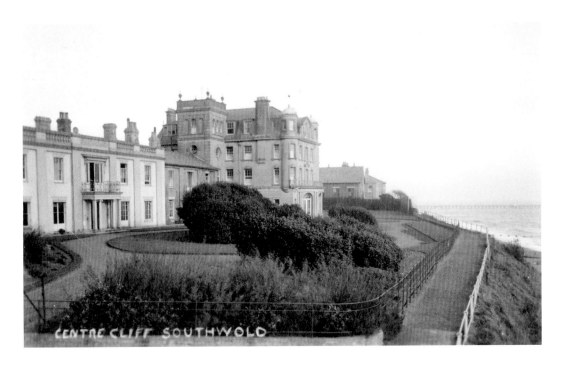

Centre Cliff

The Centre Cliff Hotel was one of the earliest of Southwold's large seafront hotels. It was opened by Adnams, the local brewers, in 1887. In 1899 a new wing was added, giving an additional thirty bedrooms. Just along from the hotel is the Sailors' Reading Room, built in 1864 in memory of Captain Rayley, which today is a fascinating, small seafaring museum and social centre for fishermen, coastguards and lifeboatmen.

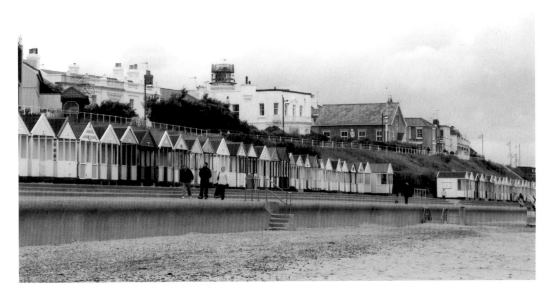

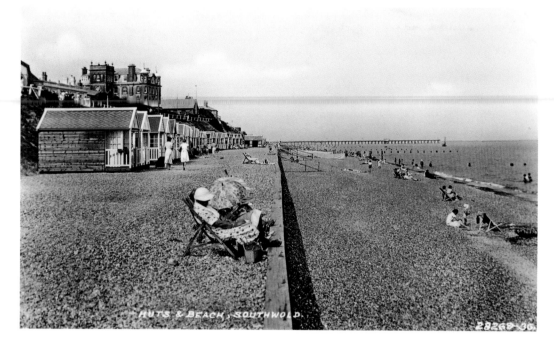

Huts and Beach

Southwold and beach huts go together like sand and sea. Brightly coloured, they line the bottom of the cliff below Centre Cliff in this mid-1930s photograph. They are protected by a low wooden sea defence. For towns like Southwold, the battle against the sea is never-ending. Below is a photograph from the late 1930s, used as a postcard in August 1945. It is from a son to his mum and part of the message reads, 'Evie has bought a pair of useless field glasses for 10 shillings. Yours in despair'.

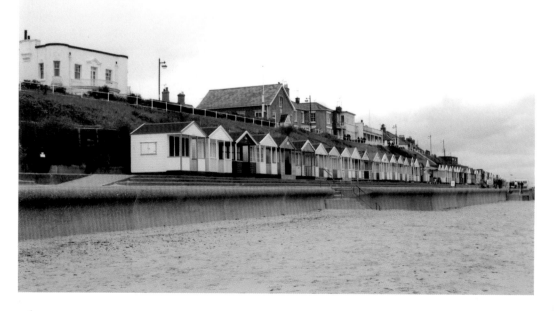

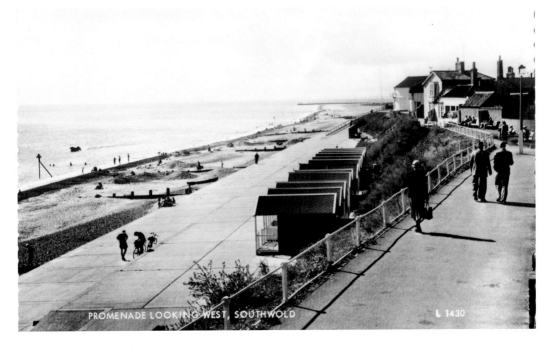

Promenade Looking West

Walking along the beach will take you to the harbour mouth, while the cliff top walk curves round towards Gun Hill. Either way it is a beautiful walk with stunning views of the coastline. While you walk, if you don't own one you can contemplate that one of the earliest beach huts, measuring just 7 feet square, went on the market in 2011 for £60,000. There is a Beach Hut Owners Association and renting one out for a week can cost between £125 and £200.

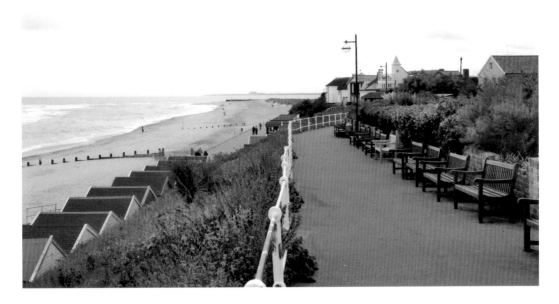

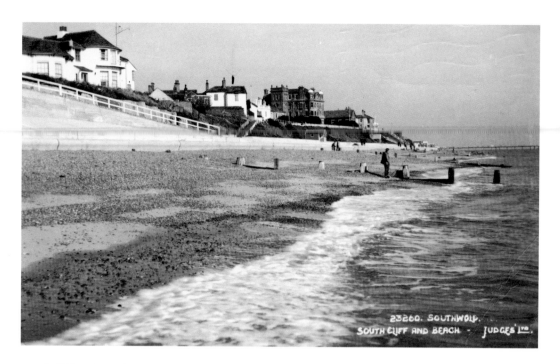

Southcliff and Beach

In this early 1920s photograph visitors are returning to the town after the First World War , during which there had been a great fear of invasion and the holidaymakers had gone. Belgian refugees had arrived and troops were billeted in the town and all over the Common. There were zeppelin raids too; one was shot down and crashed at Theberton, while in 1917 there was a brief bombardment from the sea. It was said that the guns from Flanders could be heard in Southwold.

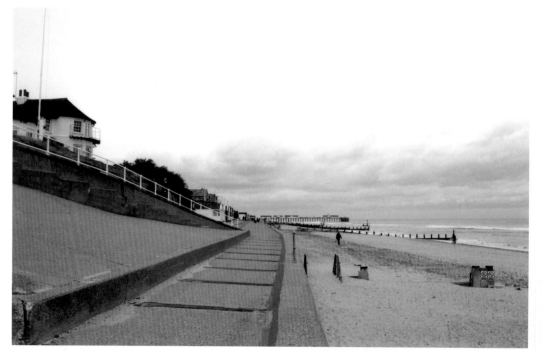

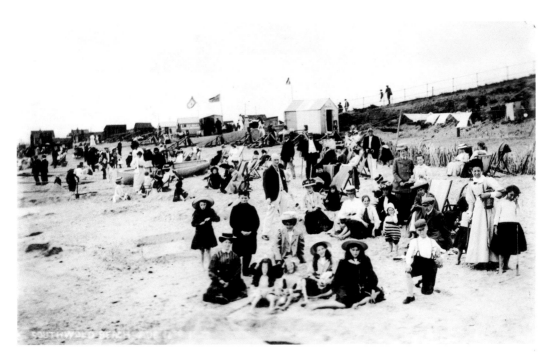

Southwold Beach

A popular stretch of sands past Gun Hill captured in Edwardian times. The postcard was written in September 1907 from a 'Loving Father' to his 'Dearest Boy', who he hopes is settling in at the Congregational School in Caterham. He tells him that his mother will send him stamps when she writes and that the weather that day has been 'dull and cold'. One feels for the recipient as the lovely photograph seems enough to make any boy homesick and yearn for the summer just past.

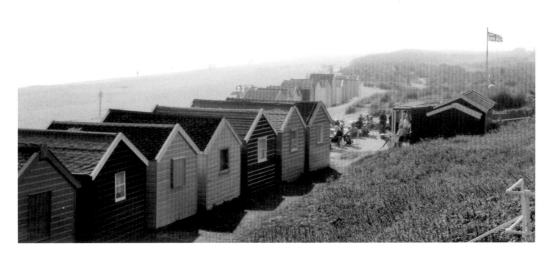

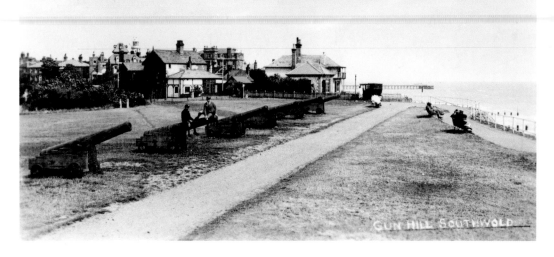

Gun Hill

Legend has it that the cannon on Gun Hill were presented to the town by the Duke of Cumberland after the defeat of Bonnie Prince Charlie at the Battle of Culloden in 1745. It seems more likely that they were given by the Royal Ordnance to protect Southwold from the Dunkirk pirates. In the First World War the Germans declared that these guns made Southwold a 'fortified place' and shelled the town. During the Second World War the guns were removed and buried so that the Germans did not think that Southwold was a legitimate military target, although two 6-inch guns were installed nearby to respond to any naval attacks.

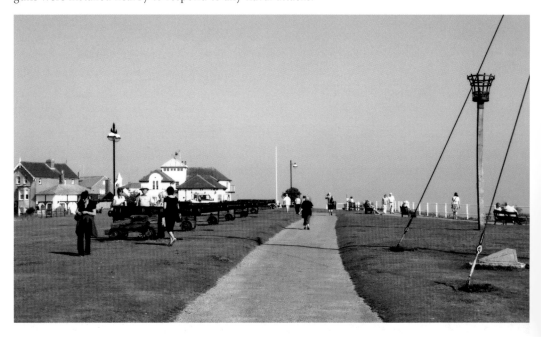

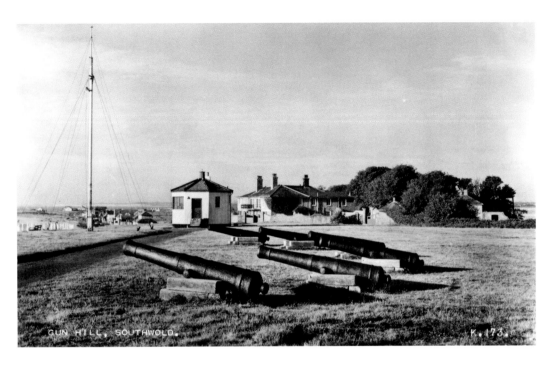

Gun Hill

A later view showing the old gun carriages. The wheels have been replaced and the cannon are no longer in a straight line as they are again today, on new carriages made locally. The quaint casino building, with its panoramic view of the coast, was once a reading room. It is now the home of Blyth Valley Community Radio. Before the guns arrived the hill was known as Eye Hill.

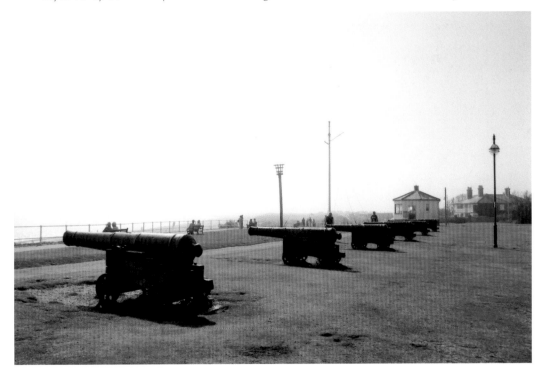

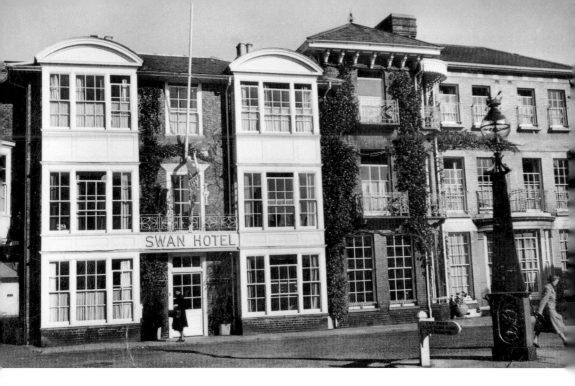

Swan Hotel

The beautiful Swan Hotel on the market place is on the site of an old brewhouse that was destroyed in the fire of 1659. The inn was rebuilt but the brewhouse moved to a site at the rear of it. In 1818 Thomas Blokenham bought the Swan and built the fine town house next to it, now part of the hotel. The brewhouse was sold to William Crisp who established the Sole Bay Brewery. In 1872 George and Ernest Adnams arrived in Southwold from Berkshire, bought the brewery and established Adnams Ales. There are organised tours of the brewery with a chance to sample the local product.

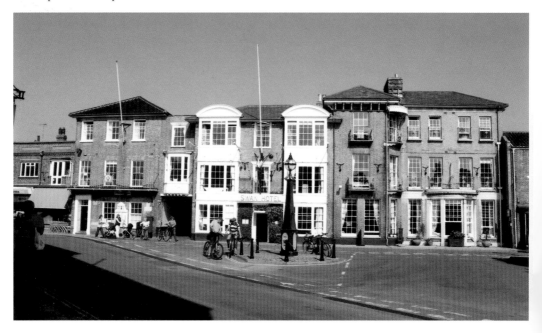

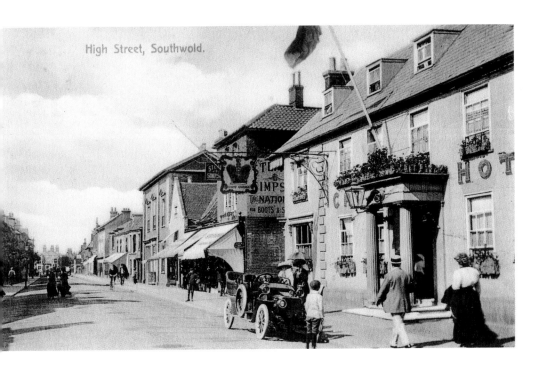

Crown Hotel

The eighteenth-century Crown Hotel in the busy High Street is an award-winning pub and small hotel, with fourteen rooms. It is part of the Adnams group. A listed building, it has been sympathetically extended over the years, taking in the next door property, but retains many of its original features.

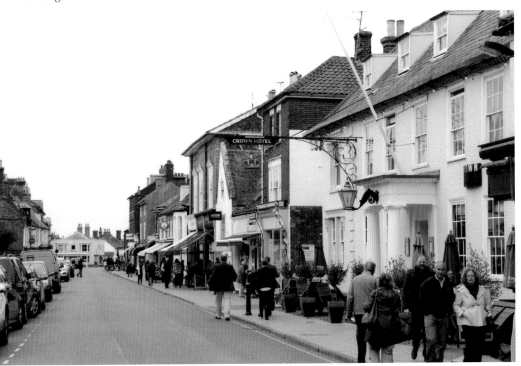

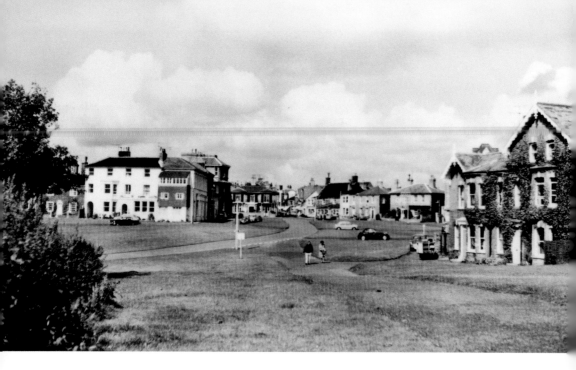

South Green

Fine houses overlook the South Green just off the East Cliff and linking through to Queen Street and the High Street. The green is crossed by the road leading down to the harbour. There is a spaciousness about here as Southwold opens up towards the common. The fire that destroyed so many buildings in 1659 led to the town being laid out around such green spaces.

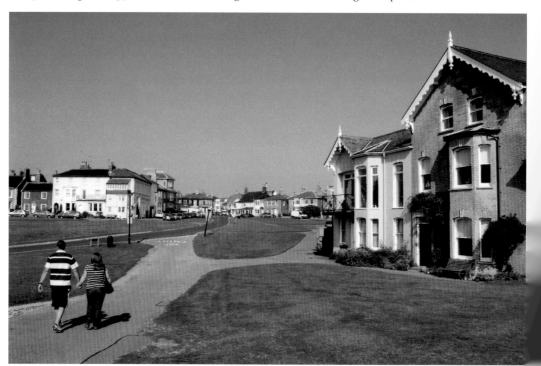

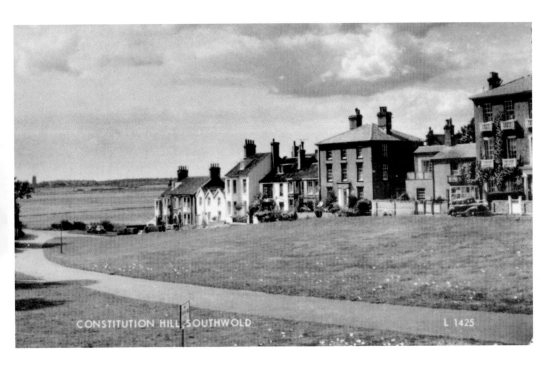

Constitution Hill

The road leads down to the marshes and the harbour. It is the openness of the common and the marshes around Southwold that contribute to its reputation for healthy air. Effectively Southwold is a small island, with the sea on one side, Buss Creek to the north-west and the River Blyth to the south- west. During the great flood of 1953 water swept in from the north and the south, cutting off the town.

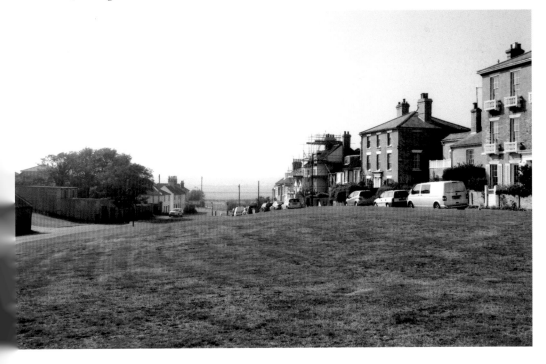

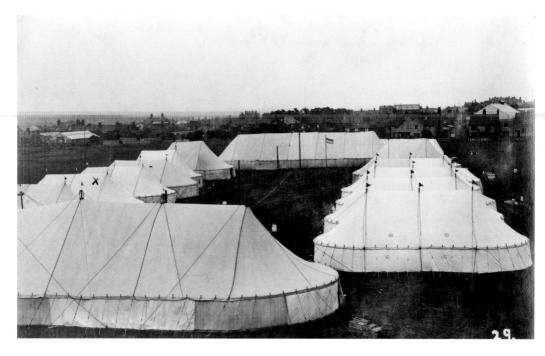

The Common

The Common is described as the 'playground of Southwold'. It stretches for some 140 acres and was given to the townspeople by William Godell, a local merchant, in 1509. It is a wonderful open recreational space and the home to many clubs for organised sport. A golf club was founded in 1894. Between 1931 and 1938 it was the site for the Duke of York's camp. The Duke, who was to become King George VI, established his camps for boys from all backgrounds in 1921 and when the camp was at Southwold he was a regular visitor.

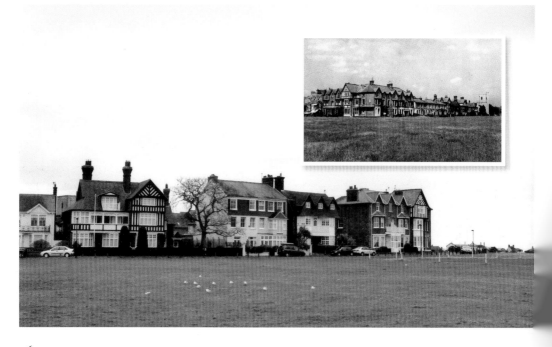

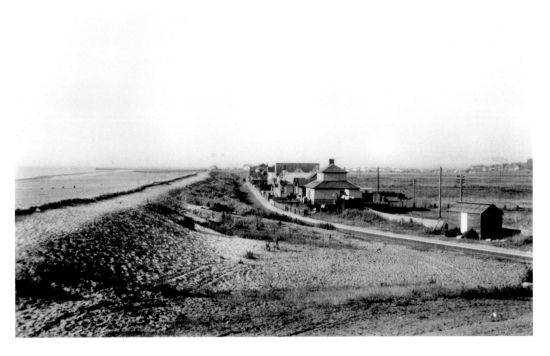

Ferry Road

Formerly known as Harbour Road, it runs parallel with the South beach down to the harbour. There is a small yacht pond halfway along, and the lifeboat house used to be opposite on the beach but is now on the north pier of the harbour mouth. Ferry Road was badly hit by the 1953 floods and many properties were destroyed, with the loss of several lives. Near the harbour there was an octagonal fish market built in the early 1900s, which was known locally as 'the Kipperdrome'. Sadly, with the decline of the industry it did not survive long. Today there is a large caravan park for holidaymakers.

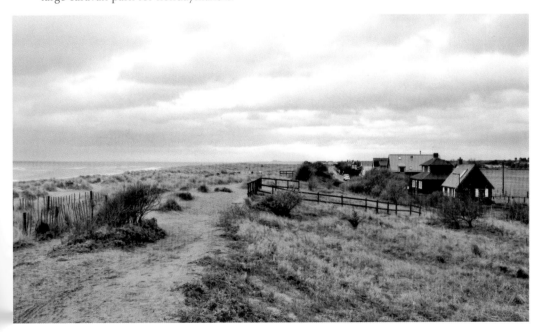

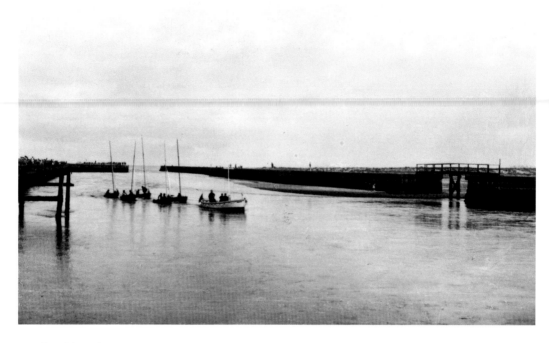

Southwold Harbour

In 1586, Camden's described Southwold: '[It] lyes in a plain low and open, expos'd to the sea; which the conveniences of the harbour, made by the River Blith's unloading itself there, has render'd a pretty populous town. At high water it is so encompest with the Sea, that you'd take it for an Island, and wonder that 'tis not all overflow'd.' Fishing and boatbuilding were Southwold's main industries. In the time of Henry VIII the port competed with Dunwich, Covehithe and Walberswick for the Icelandic fishing trade.

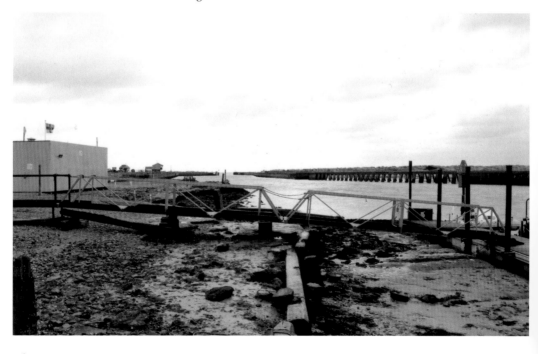

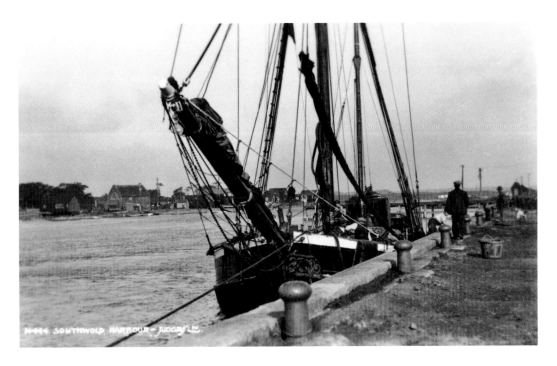

Southwold Harbour

In Victorian times hundreds of vessels arrived and sailed from the port. In 1906 the harbour was sold by the Corporation to the Southwold Harbour Company. There was an expensive reconstruction in the hope of challenging Lowestoft and Great Yarmouth for the herring fishing. The port suffered from periods of decline because of silting up but these extensive harbour works brought a period of prosperity. In 1908 just 300 fishing boats used the harbour but by 1909 there were 761, including seventy Scots luggers, bringing with them the Scots girls who gutted and prepared the herring.

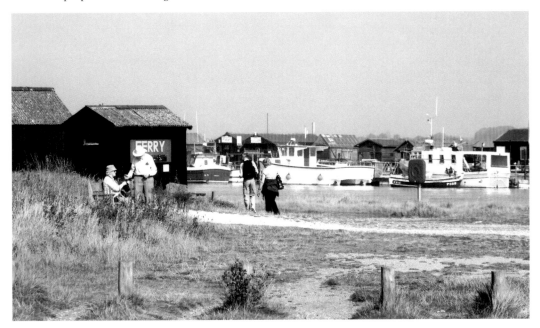

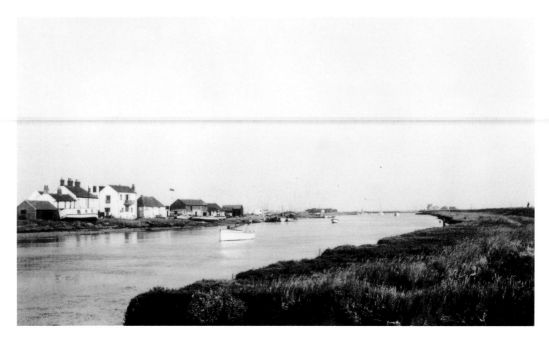

River Blyth

A railway branch line to the harbour was opened in 1913, but the business was in decline and the First World War saw further loss of trade. In 1933 the harbour reverted to the Corporation and is busy again with pleasure craft of all sizes. The banks of the Blyth are popular with walkers. There is a bailey bridge across the river where there was once a swing bridge carrying the railway. The track bed is now a cycle route. This is a charming and popular area, always bustling with life. The Harbour Inn has a high water mark above its door showing how badly the harbour was hit by the 1953 floods.

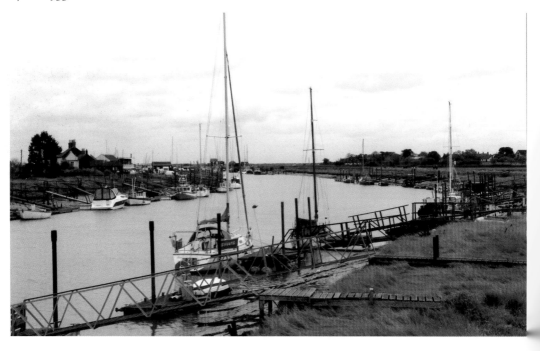

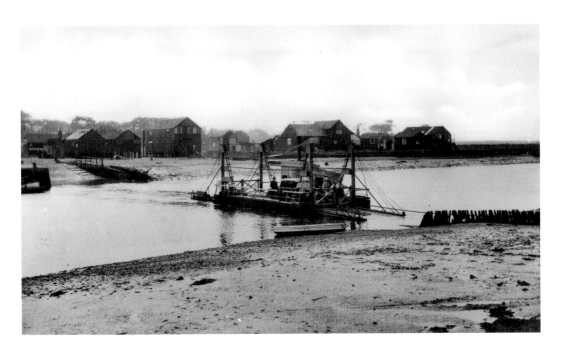

Walberswick Ferry

There have been many ferries across the Blyth, dating back to the thirteenth century. In 1885 the River Blyth Ferry Company was set up and in 1889 they invested in a hand-cranked pontoon capable of carrying bigger loads. In 1927 this was replaced by a steam ferry, *The Blyth*, seen here carrying a car. It even famously transported a circus elephant. The steam ferry ceased operating in 1942. Today there is a seasonal ferry powered by an outboard motor. By road the journey is 7 miles!

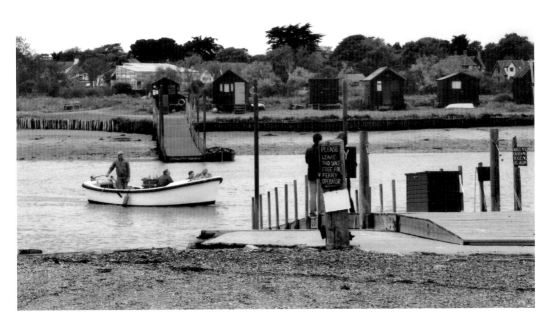

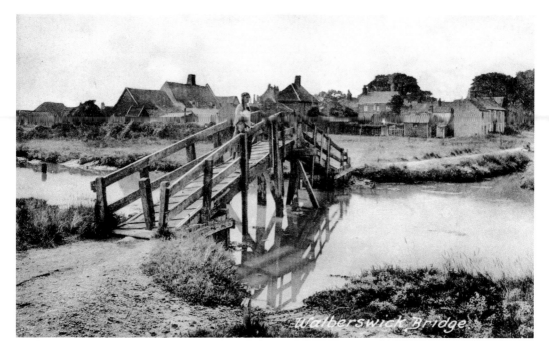

Walberswick Bridge

Photographed in the 1920s and known as the Kissing Bridge, it now takes walkers across the small creek running in from the Blyth and to the harbour wall or down to the sands and the sea. Walberswick is a very popular spot for crabbing and from 1982 to 2010 hosted the British Open Crabbing Championships. The extraordinary success of the event, with 1252 entrants in 2009 and another very busy year in 2010, overwhelmed the village, so much so that no event was held in 2011.

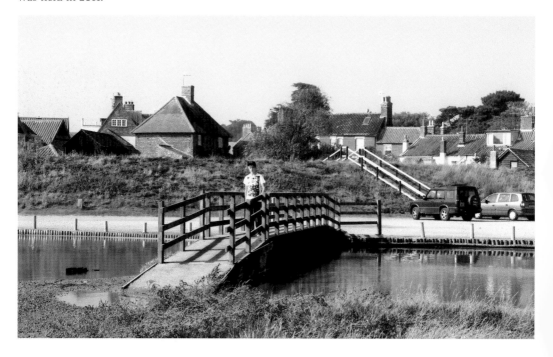

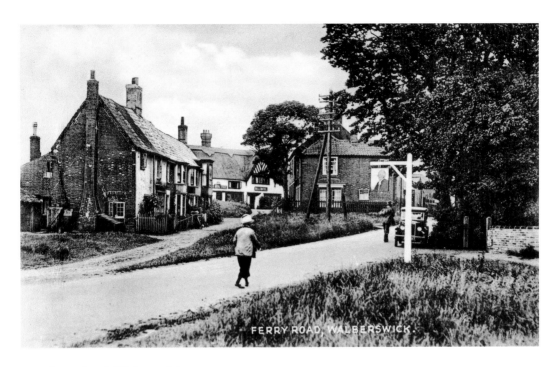

Ferry Road, Walberswick

Walberswick is a fascinating village and very popular with artists, holidaymakers, trippers and walkers. It is also very popular for those who can afford a second home. It was once a thriving port with a trade in fish, cheese, corn, bacon and timber, but as with Southwold the trade declined after the First World War. Many of the old fishermen's huts and houses on stilts were swept away in the great storm that hit the coast in 1953, but it is still a delightful village.

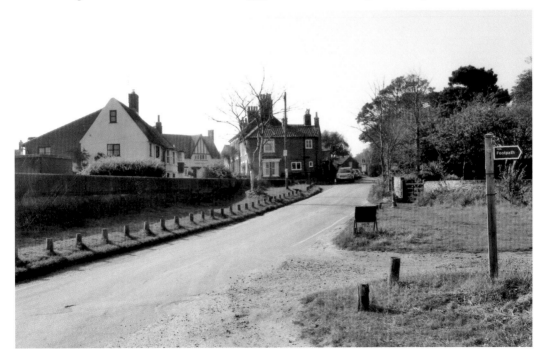

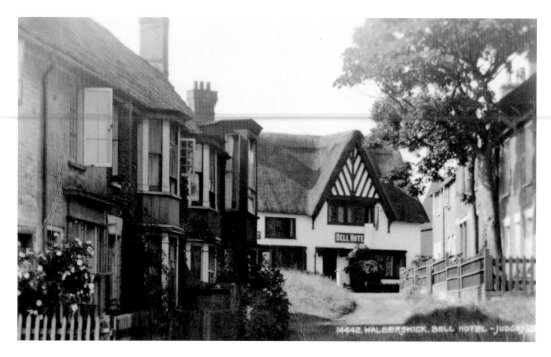

Walberswick Bell Hotel

Janet sent this card in late September 1956 to Chingford: 'Have come to Southwold for day and paddled along to W'wick – this shows a small part of Bell Hotel – it looks so very lovely. It is terrifically hot, in fact a super day.'

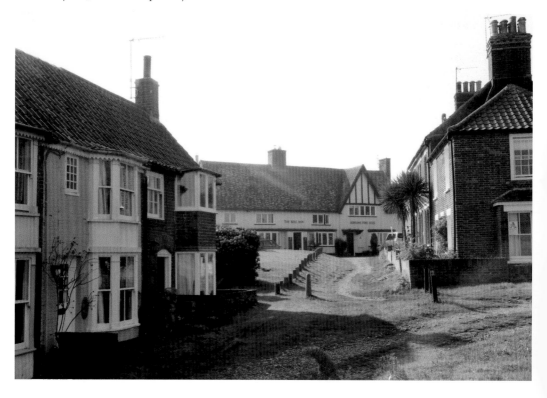

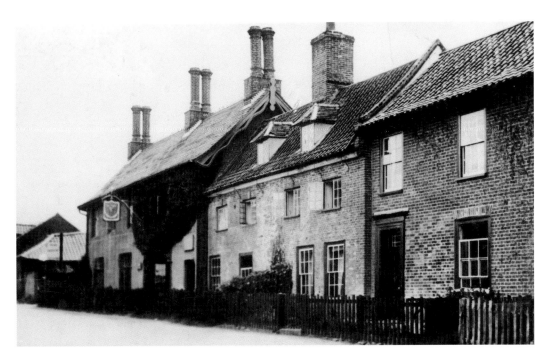

The Barne Arms Hotel, Dunwich

Still very recognisable, along the road to the beach and close to the small museum, the Barne Arms has reverted to its original name of the Ship. The Ship Inn probably dates from the sixteenth century. The Barne family, who were merchants in the City of London, bought the Dunwich estate in 1754 and later changed the inn's name. The family sold their principal residence, Greyfriars, and the estate in 1947. Subsequently the Barne Arms became the Ship again.

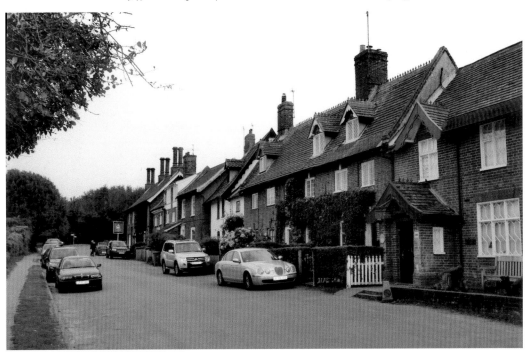

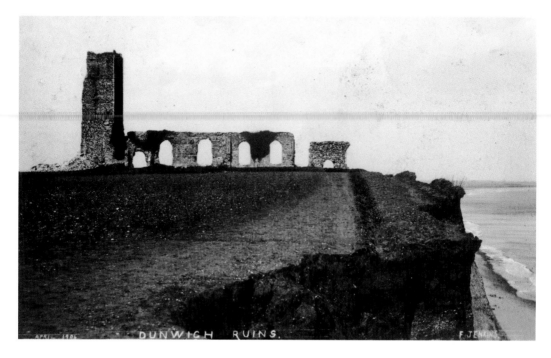

Dunwich Ruins, 1904

Dunwich is sometimes described as 'Britain's Atlantis', for what was once one of the most important medieval towns in the country has now been swallowed up by the relentless sea. The most iconic of the ruins was that of All Saints church. In Victorian times and the early years of the twentieth century visitors, including writers like Edward Fitzgerald, Thomas Carlyle and Algernon Swinburne, were drawn to the village, along with artists like Turner. In April 1904, this photograph carries the message, 'This photograph was taken this month, so you can see what a lot of the cliffs have fallen since last year.'

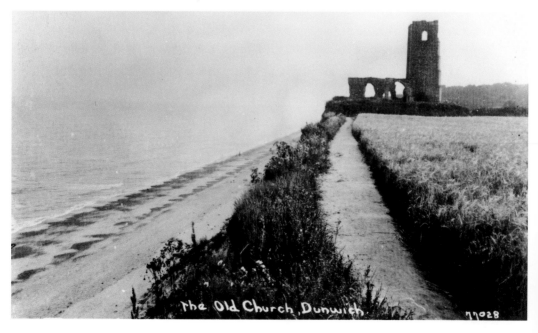

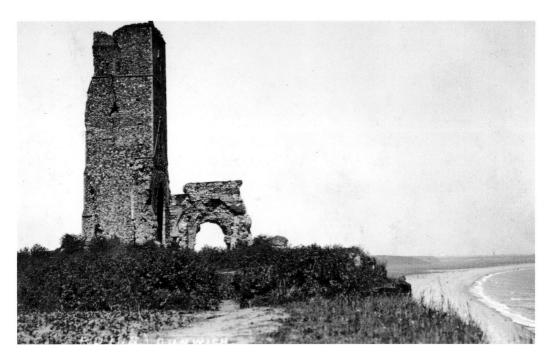

Dunwich

By 1910 All Saints was even nearer the edge and in 1919 the church finally fell into the sea. It is said that from the thirteenth century at least seven churches and the Blackfriars monastery were lost to the sea. Camden wrote of Dunwich, in his *Britannia* of 1586: 'But now by a private pique of Nature (which has set no fixt bounds to the incursions of the Sea) the greatest part of it is swept away by the violence of the waves...it lies now in solitude and desolation.'

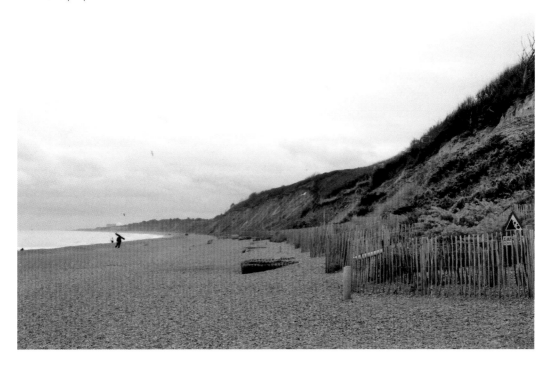

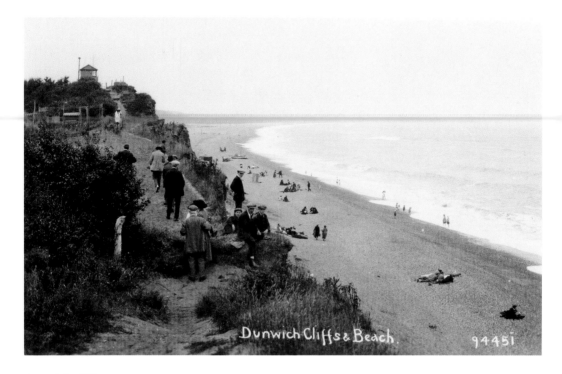

Dunwich Cliffs & Beach. 94451

Dunwich Cliffs, *c.* 1919

In 1086 Dunwich was one of the ten largest towns or cities in England. At one time it was the seat of the first Bishop of East Anglia and held Royal Charters for a market and a mint. The wealth came from sea trade and fishing, but Dunwich faced two major problems. The port was silting up and the coast was eroding at frightening speed. Today there are some 120 inhabitants of Dunwich, with a large car park and tea room giving easy access to the beach and the crumbling cliffs.

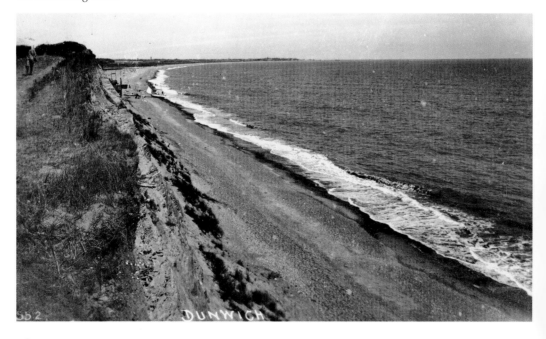

DUNWICH

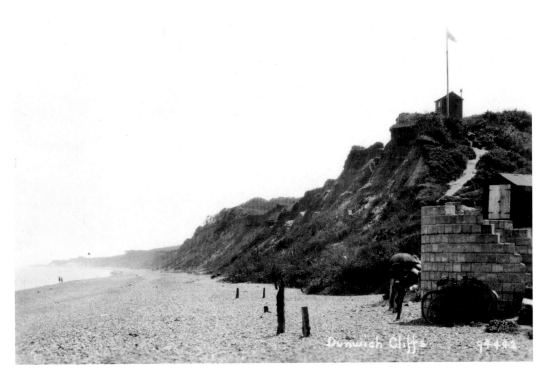

Dunwich Cliffs

These three photographs all appear to date from about 1920 and the church has finally gone. Pieces of wall or foundation can be seen on the cliff edge. One of them, posted in 1919 to Felixstowe, carries the words, 'so glad you are having such a ripping time'.

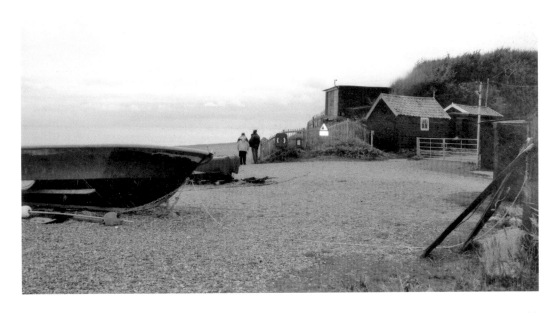

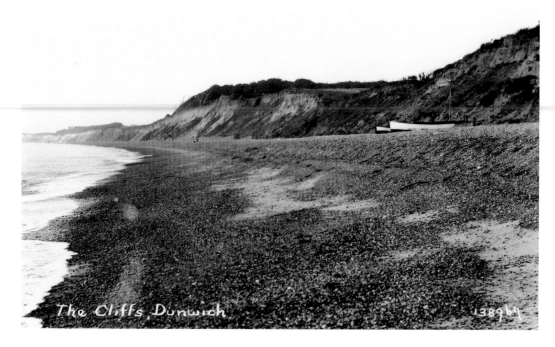

The Cliffs, Dunwich, *c.* 1954

This is an area of outstanding national beauty on the Suffolk Heritage Coast. Walking along the beach, fences and warning signs keep us away from the cliffs. There are signs everywhere of attempts to stop the erosion. The sea has pushed the shingle up into a bank that it is a struggle to climb over. In each direction there is a gentle curve of coastline and miles and miles of almost deserted beach.

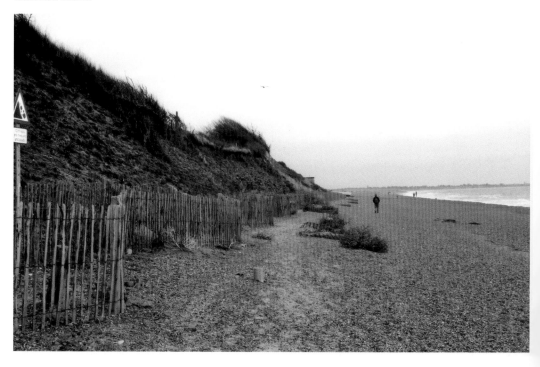

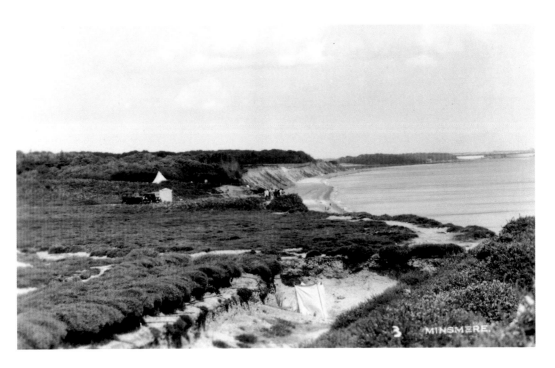

Minsmere

South of Dunwich there are several caravan parks along the cliff top, quite hidden by the trees. The Cliff House Holiday Park is clustered in among the trees around the old house, which was built as a merchant's home in the 1830s. There are wooden lodges and caravans with a modern clubhouse. There are steps down the crumbling red cliffs to the beach. The site is surrounded by National Trust land. The Royal Society for the Protection of Birds has an important reserve along the coast at Minsmere.

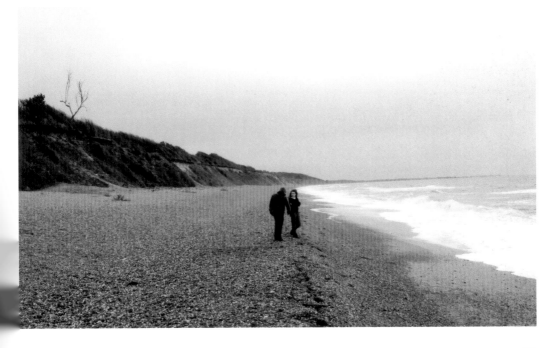

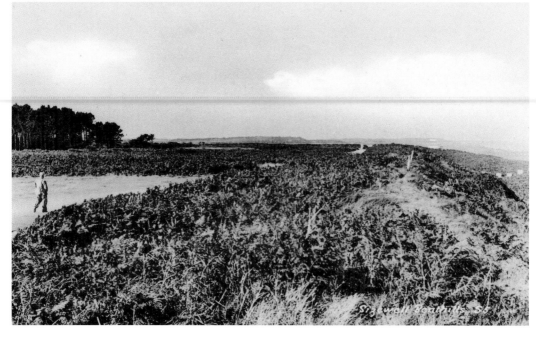

Sizewell

Sizewell is a small fishing village two miles from Leiston, but best known for the Sizewell A and B nuclear power stations built in the 1960s. The Magnox Sizewell A was shut down in 2006 and is in the process of being decommissioned, while EDF Energy is planning a new power station next to Sizewell B. There is a campaign to close this and all other nuclear power stations. Sizewell village was part of the Ogilvie estate, the Ogilvie family having bought Sizewell Hall in 1859. Today the hall is rented out as a Christian conference centre.

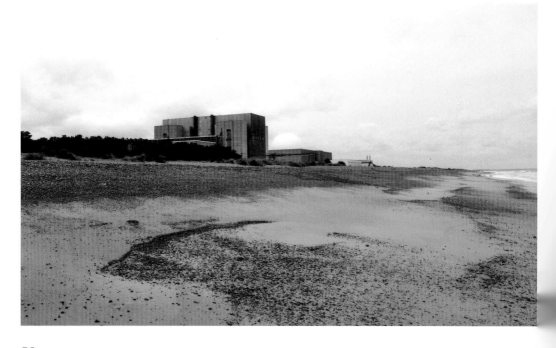

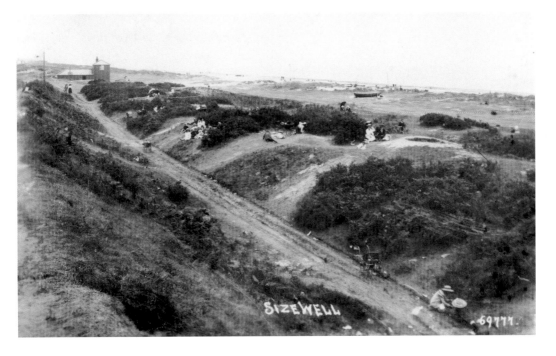

Sizewell

This is a beautiful stretch of coast and the scene of a remarkable wartime episode. Thirty-two young Dutchmen attempted to kayak across the North Sea to England to join the allied fight against Germany. Only eight reached the English shore in September 1941 and, of them, only three survived the war. A memorial of three oars, one of them broken and bearing an inscription telling of the heroic event, was erected by the path to the beach in 2009.

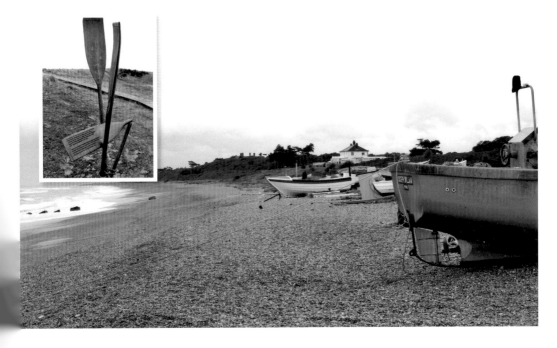

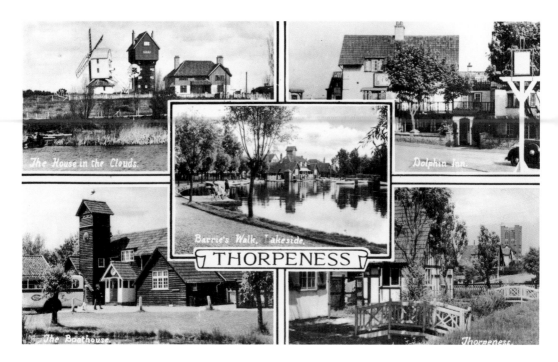

The House in the Clouds · Dolphin Inn · Barrie's Walk, Lakeside · THORPENESS · The Boathouse · Thorpeness

Thorpeness

In 1903, Glencairn Stuart Ogilvie inherited the estate stretching from Sizewell to Aldeburgh. He was a man of many parts: barrister, builder of railways and playwright. In 1910 he had the vision to create a holiday village. He planned to provide self-catering family holidays. Seaside Bungalows Limited was formed but this soon changed to Thorpeness Limited. Everything was planned by Ogilvie to create an olde-worlde English village by the sea. His architect was Frederick Forbes Glennie.

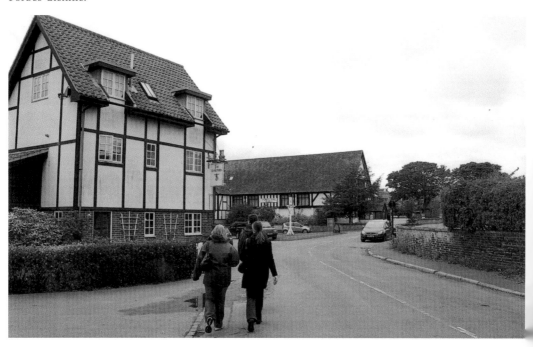

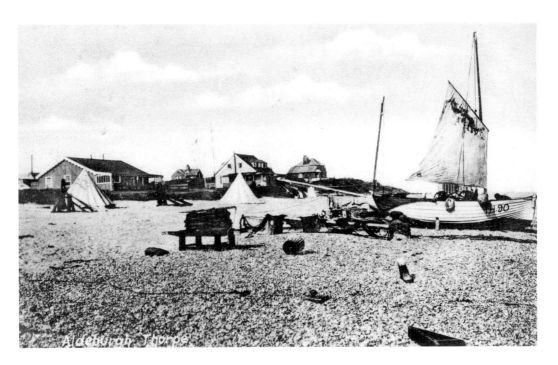

Aldeburgh Thorpe, *c.* 1908

When Glencairn Stuart Ogilvie acquired the estate there was a small village of Thorpe, part of the parish of Aldringham-cum-Thorpe, with the Dolphin Inn. Bungalows and houses were perched near the sea, as this early photograph shows. In fact the bungalow in the foreground was wrecked in violent storms and high tide in 1911. That tide not only washed away some bungalows but also some of the sandhills to reveal various old coins and artefacts.

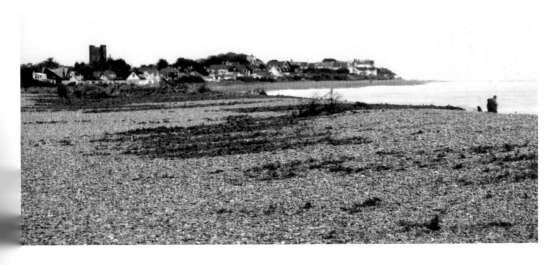

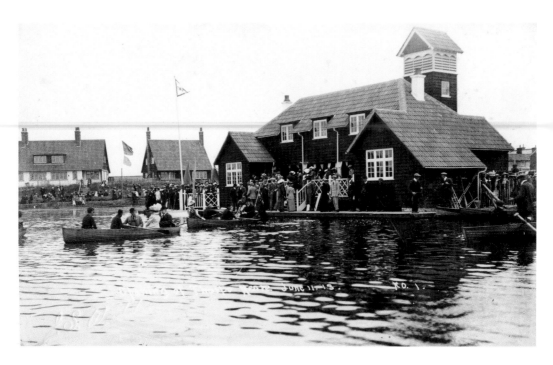

Opening of the Meare, 1913

In November 1910 there was extensive flooding at Thorpe and it is said that Ogilvie, in looking at the vast area of water, said 'let's keep it and build a holiday village around it.' Whatever its origins, the Meare, which is fed by the Hundred River, is sixty-four acres of artificial lake no more than three feet deep. It is a wonderfully safe boating lake with a number of islands called after places in *Peter Pan*, like 'Pirates' Lair' and 'Wendy's Home'.

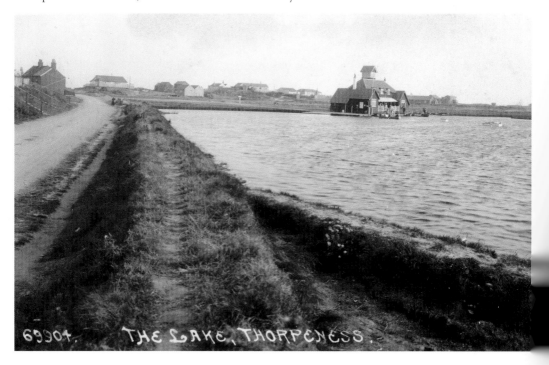

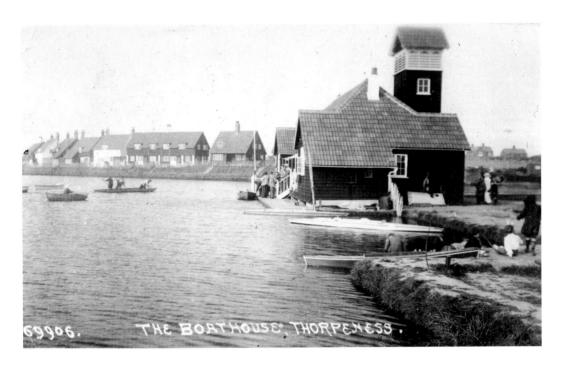

The Boathouse

The Boathouse was one of the earliest buildings in Thorpeness, built in 1911. It was open before the Meare was ready for its official opening. All manner of boats may be hired to take out on the Meare. The Meare is the home of the Thorpeness Regatta every August.

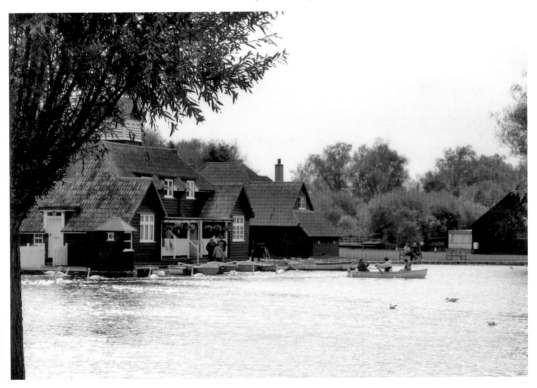

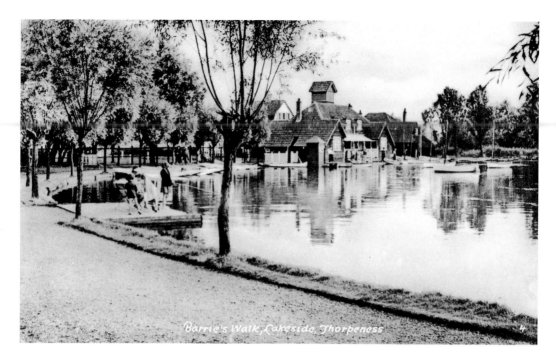

Barrie's Walk, Lakeside, Thorpeness

Barrie's Walk

The path that winds round alongside the Meare was named Barrie's Walk in honour of J. M. Barrie, who was a frequent visitor to Thorpeness and a personal friend of Glencairn Stuart Ogilvie. It is easy to see the influence of Barrie's *Peter Pan* in what Ogilvie was trying to create – a Neverland for holidaymakers. The estate would manage everything. This was a village designed for families to stay with their maids. Barrie's play of *Peter Pan* premiered in 1904 and a novel version of the story was published in 1911, just as Ogilvie was creating Thorpeness.

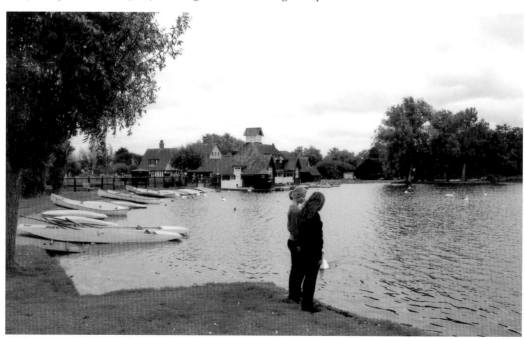

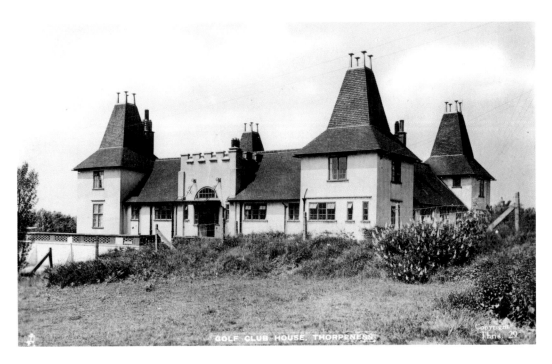

Golf Club House

The golf club, with each of its turrets tipped with four giant golf tees, was built in 1930. It is now known as the Thorpeness Hotel. The course itself was designed by James Braid in 1922. It is an 18-hole course set in the glorious coastal heathlands.

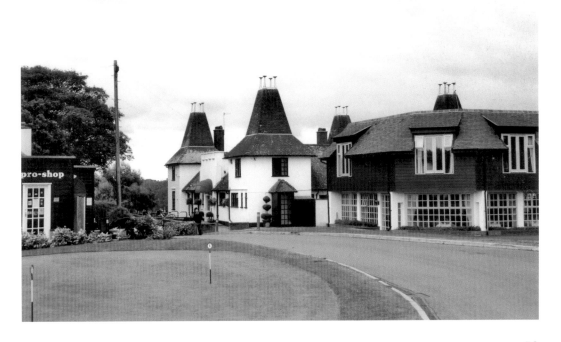

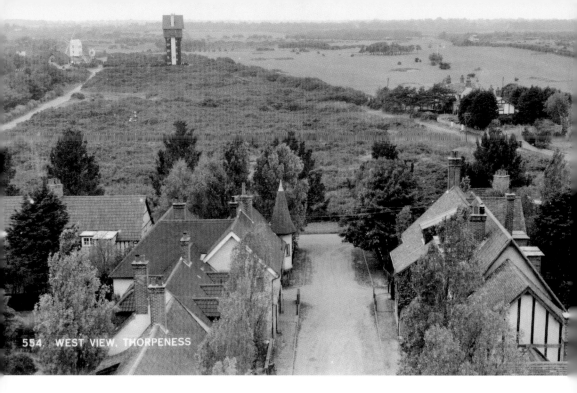

554. WEST VIEW, THORPENESS

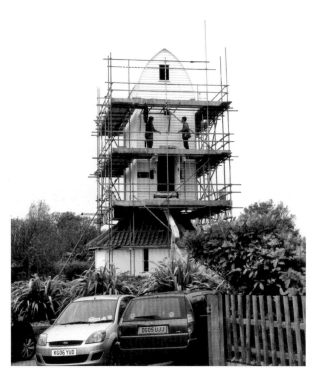

West View of Thorpeness

A windmill is an essential element in any recreation of 'Merrie England'. If you haven't got one, find one and move it. The Thorpeness windmill was a corn mill at Aldringham and it was moved to its present site in the early 1920s to pump water into the top of the water tank. On my visit in September 2011 it was being renovated. The mill is a Heritage Coast Centre.

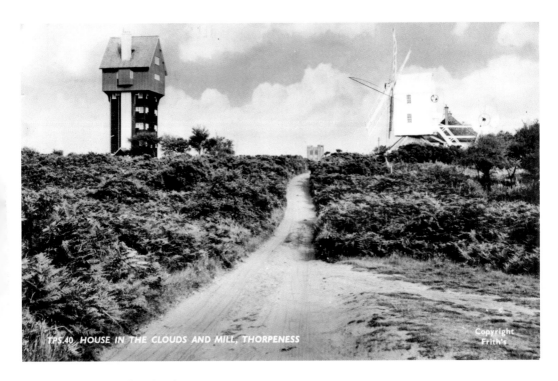

TPS.40. HOUSE IN THE CLOUDS AND MILL, THORPENESS

Copyright
Frith's

The House in the Clouds

Possibly the most remarkable of all Thorpeness' eccentricities is the 'House in the Clouds'. It was built as a water tank in 1923. It was a writer of children's books, Mrs Malcolm Mason, who suggested to Mr Ogilvie that he should disguise the water tank, board in the steel structure and provide accommodation. He did so and she became the first tenant. Today it is a very popular holiday let.

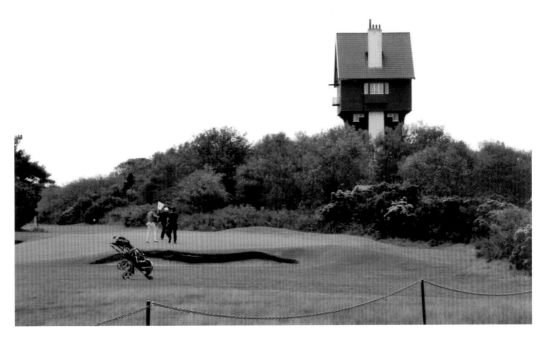

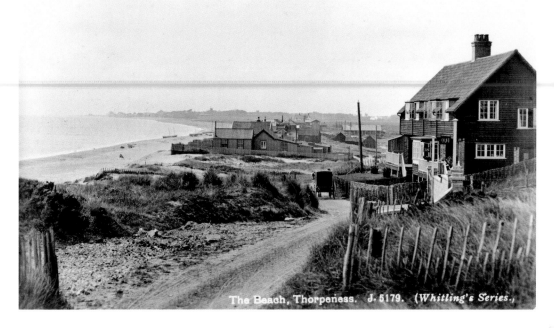

The Beach, Thorpeness. J. 5179. (*Whitling's Series.*)

The Beach

The Saxmundham to Aldeburgh railway line ran close by and a halt was soon provided at Thorpeness for visitors to the new holiday village. Three Great Eastern passenger coaches were acquired as station buildings and they remained as such until the line was axed in 1966. This photograph dates from soon after development began at Thorpeness and as the sender writes: 'There are several boarding houses here to let – plenty of windows, just what we have been looking for.'

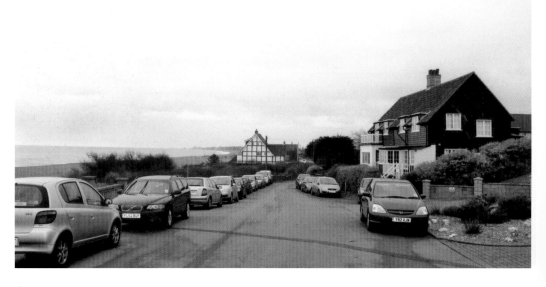

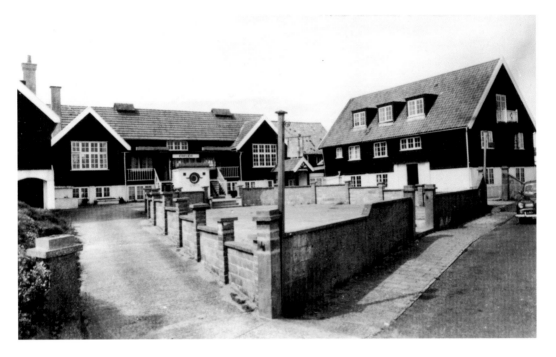

The Country Club

The Country Club opened in 1912. During the First World War it was commandeered for troops and so badly damaged that after the war it had to be to be reconstructed. Gradually it has been added to over the years. For tennis lovers there are six hard tennis courts and three grass courts in summer.

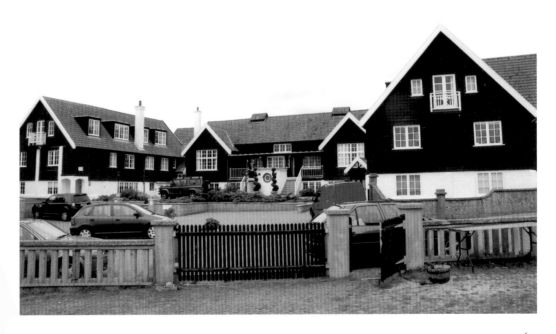

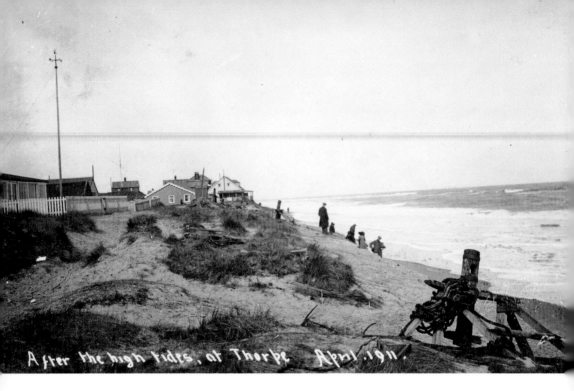

After the high tides, at Thorpe April 1911.

The Beach, Thorpeness

A dramatic photograph showing some of the damage done by that high tide of April 1911. Despite the ever-present risk Ogilvie developed his village. Looking at the photograph below you can see what the earlier writer meant by 'plenty of windows'!

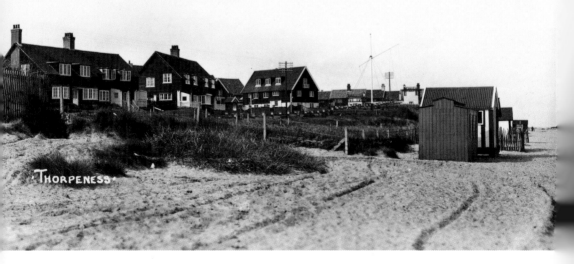

.THORPENESS.

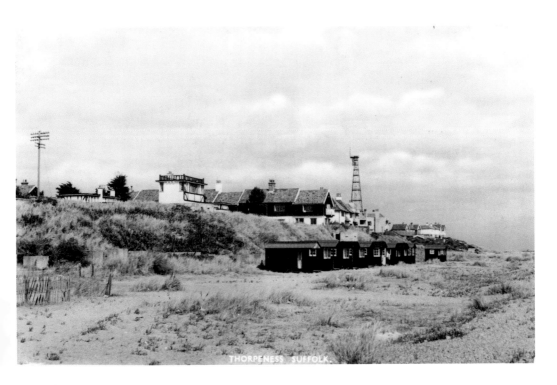

Thorpeness, c. 1950

Beach huts nestle at the foot of the low grass-covered cliff, while in the background can be seen the tower of the wartime radar station. It was erected in 1942 as part of the chain of stations along the coast. This part of the coast was in the front line of defence in the event of invasion from 1940. In the 1970s and '80s the Ogilvie estate was broken up and sold off, but the original vision survives to give pleasure to today's holidaymakers and fascinate visitors.

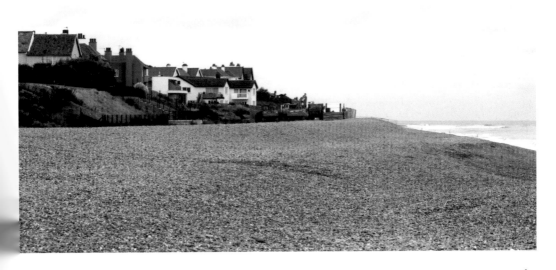

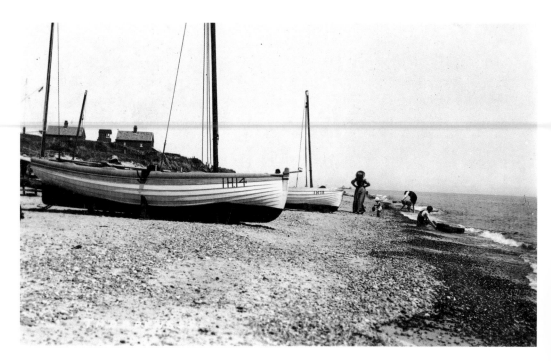

Thorpeness

Walking or driving between Aldeburgh and Thorpeness and there on the shingle, facing the sea, is Suffolk-born Maggi Hambling's steel sculpture, *The Scallop*. It was erected in 2003 as a tribute to Benjamin Britten. It would be true to say that opinion was divided on its merits or position. My daughter and her friend found it irresistible, as did other children, and I've yet to see it without people of all ages around it. Maggi Hambling said: '*The Scallop* explodes out of the shingle'. I love it!

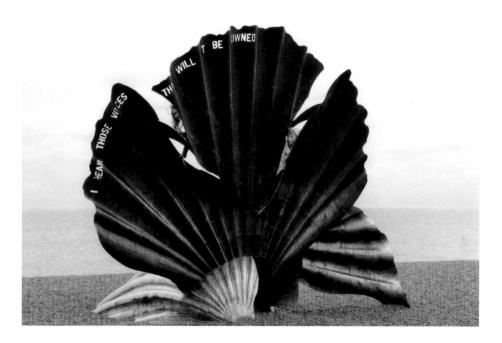

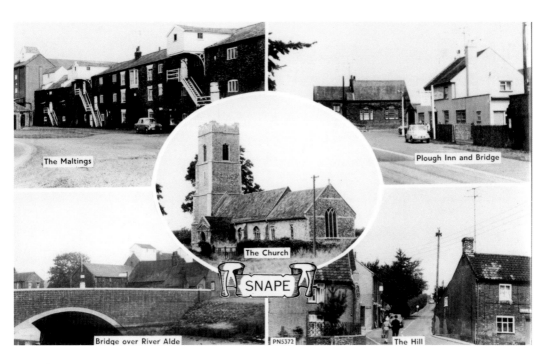

The Maltings

Plough Inn and Bridge

The Church

SNAPE

Bridge over River Alde

PN5372

The Hill

Snape

Newson Garrett (1812–1893), maltster and brewer, built the Snape Maltings beside the River Alde in the mid-1850s. He was the father of Elizabeth Garrett Anderson and also served as mayor of Aldeburgh. In 1967 Benjamin Britten and Peter Pears converted the maltings into a concert venue for the Aldeburgh Festival. In 2006 Aldeburgh Music purchased the concert hall and invested £14 million in developing the Snape venue as a cultural attraction. Today its international reputation draws holidaymakers and visitors from all over.

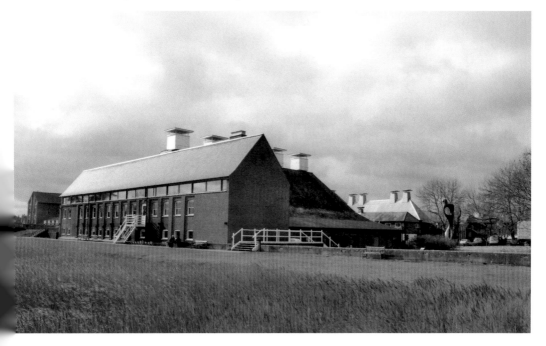

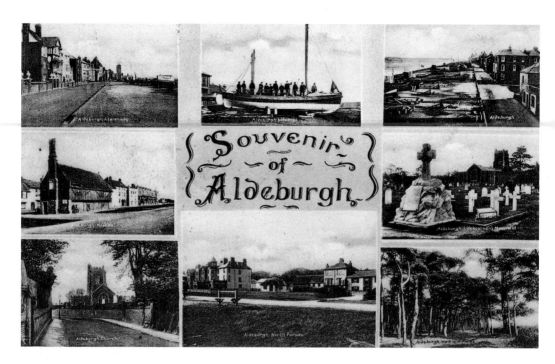

Aldeburgh

There is a timeless quality about Aldeburgh. To visit is to sense what the early seaside resorts must have once been like. There are seafront hotels, the promenade and the beach. It consists of pebble and shingle ridges constantly being pushed by the North Sea, which over the centuries claimed much of the old town. Fresh fish is sold from the beach-side shacks – as one sign says, 'Anything fresher is still swimming'. Here you feel the closeness of the relationship between man and the sea.

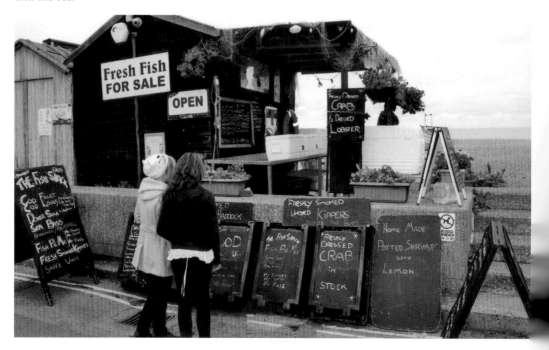

The Steps

There is a steep climb to the top of the Town Steps and the Terrace, but it is rewarding to see the rooftops spread out below and then the sea. The larger town houses were built up here, while the fishermen's cottages were at the foot, closer to the sea. The steps are a much photographed feature of Aldeburgh. C. S. Ward wrote in the early 1880s: 'It is impossible to lose one's way at Aldeburgh, and so no guidance is needed. Besides the picturesque seafront, the steep beach and the brilliant bathing machines are the most prominent objects.'

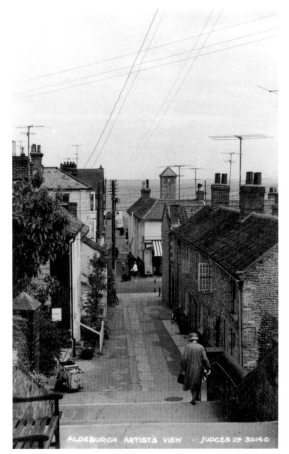

ALDEBURGH. ARTIST'S VIEW · JUDGES L⁹ 30140

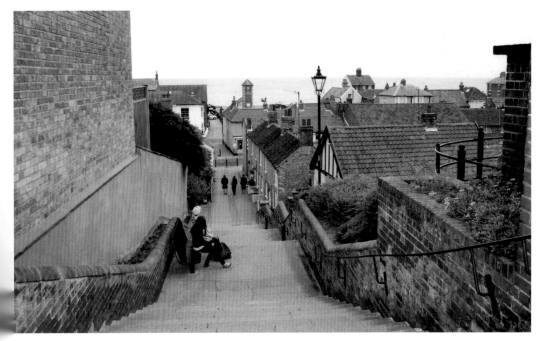

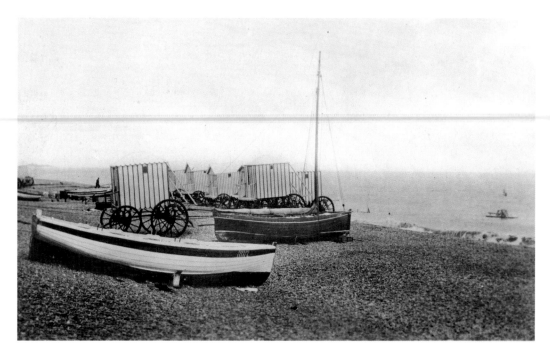

The Beach

Revd George Crabbe, in a biography of his father, the poet George Crabbe, born in Aldeburgh in 1754, described mid-eighteenth century Aldeburgh as: 'a poor and wretched place, with nothing of the elegance and gaiety which have sprung up about it, in consequence of watering parties. The town lies between a low hill or cliff, on which only the old church and a few better houses were then situated, and the beach of the German Ocean. It consisted of two parallel and unpaved streets, running between mean and scrambling houses, the abodes of seafaring men, pilots and fishers.'

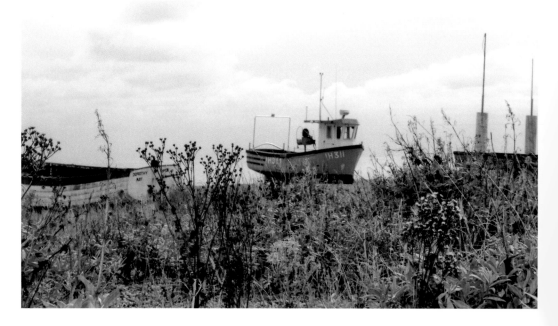

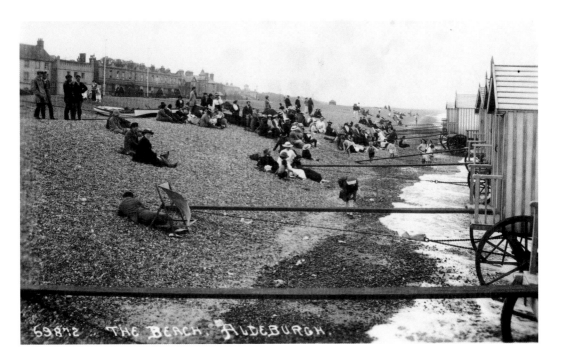

The Beach

This photograph of the beach at the northern end of Aldeburgh in the early 1920s shows a tidy line of bathing machines at the water's edge. While there is a good crowd of holidaymakers looking on, it is impossible to tell whether any are using them to take a dip. Mixed bathing was permitted at this time, but bathers were warned that 'the beach is steep at certain states of the tide and falls in a succession of steps.'

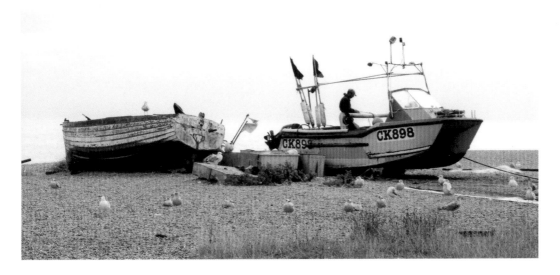

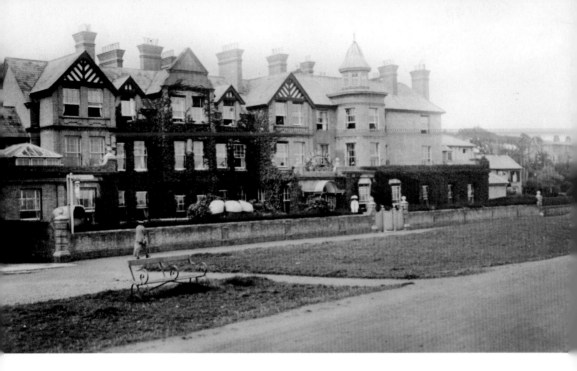

The Wentworth Hotel

The Wentworth is remarkable in that it has been managed by the Pritt family since 1920. Priding itself on 'a blend of the traditional and contemporary', it occupies a superb position on the front at the northern end of the town. It has thirty-five bedrooms and guests with a sea view can see the fish being landed on the beach from their windows. The Wentworth family were Lords of the Manor and large local landowners. When it opened in 1900 it was called the Wentworth Castle Hotel. It has changed outwardly little over the years except losing the quaint little turret.

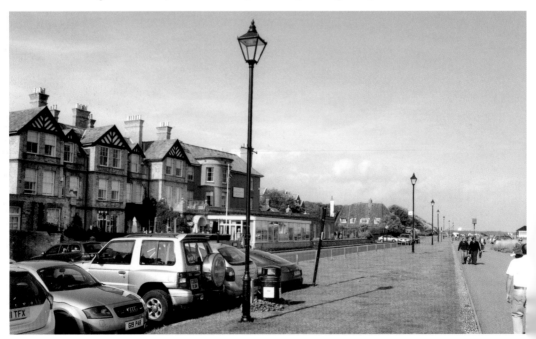

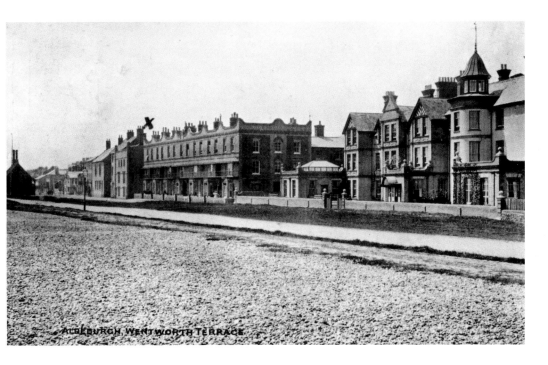

Wentworth Terrace, c. 1907

Posted in August 1907, from the postcard's inscription Hettie is obviously enjoying herself: 'What lovely weather this last few days. Such a lot of things on now, 3 or 4 different things in one day. I bathed early this morning, nearly every machine [was] full up...' Wentworth Terrace dates from the 1860s and North Lodge, which adjoined it and appears to have been built around the same time, was converted into the Wentworth Hotel.

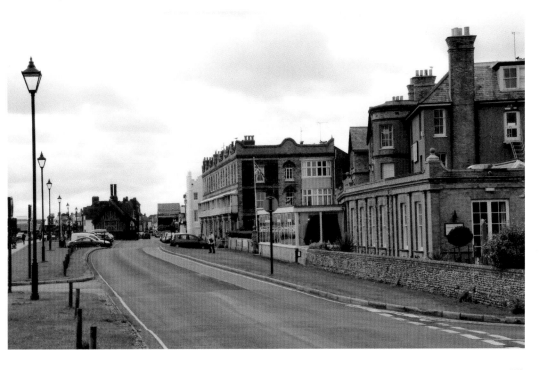

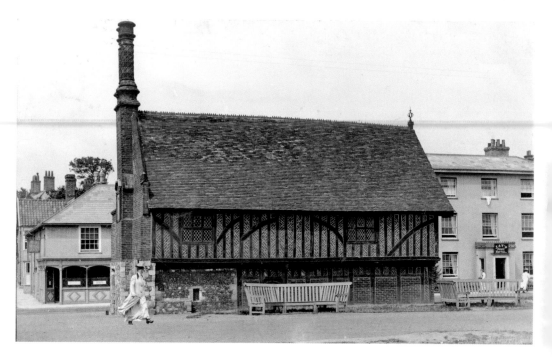

Moot Hall

Three fine photographs, probably all taken before the First World War, showing the Moot Hall, one of the most photographed buildings along the coast. The picture above is dated 1912 and shows Jay's Private Hotel in the background, while the sender remarks, 'the front is very much improved and a great many visitors'. Closer inspection of the photograph below reveals a workman on a ladder appearing over the far gable.

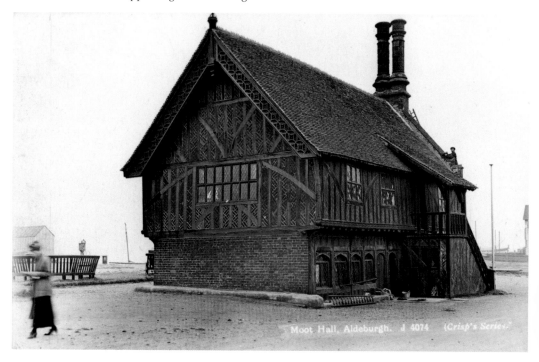

Moot Hall, Aldeburgh.   J 4074   (Crisp's Series.)

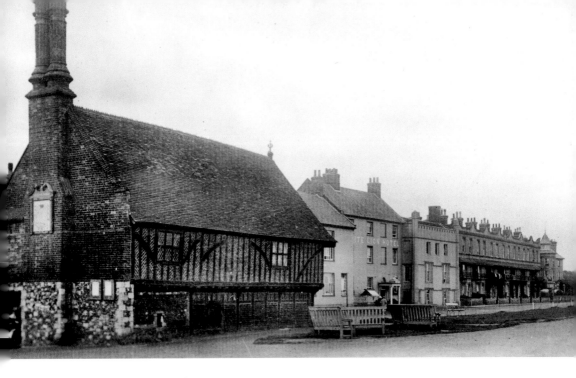

Moot Hall and Wentworth Terrace

The Moot Hall, or meeting house, had originally stood in the middle of the old town, but by the time C. S. Ward visited Aldeburgh in the 1880s the sea had claimed so many streets and buildings that it stood close to the shingle beach. Moot derives from the old English word 'mote' meaning assembly or meeting place and the building dates from at least the sixteenth century. Today, appropriately, the Town Council meets there and it is a museum, opening from April until the end of October.

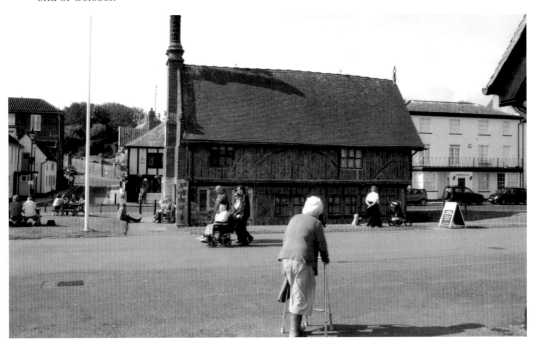

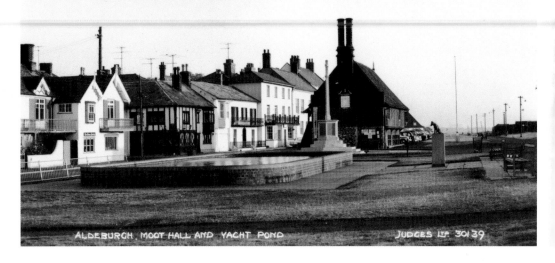

War Memorial and Moot Hall, *c.* 1935

The war memorial was unveiled in January 1921, inscribed with eighty-four names from the First World War. A further twenty-six names were added after the Second World War, including those of seven civilians. The sender of this postcard was staying at the Wentworth Hotel: 'Have had a good walk this morning along the beach into Thorpeness another old-fashioned place like this. We are very comfortable here and like the air very much, it is not so keen as I thought it would be. There are not many people in the place, the hotel has fair numbers though... bring the field glasses when you come...'

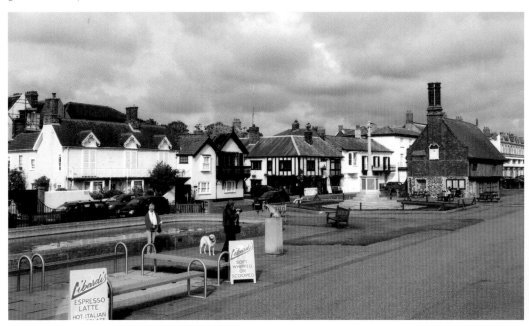

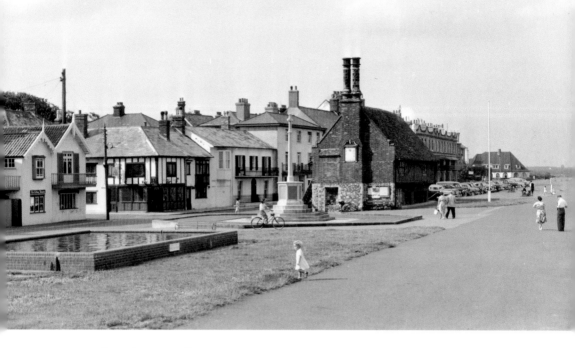

Promenade and Moot Hall

The popular model boat pond was given to the town in about 1910 by Elizabeth Garrett Anderson. She was a remarkable pioneer for women; as well as being the first female doctor in England she became Mayor of Aldeburgh in 1908, the first woman to be elected as a mayor in England. For over a hundred years now, children and adults have enjoyed the simple pleasure of wondering whether their boat will safely reach the shore or they will have to paddle to the rescue.

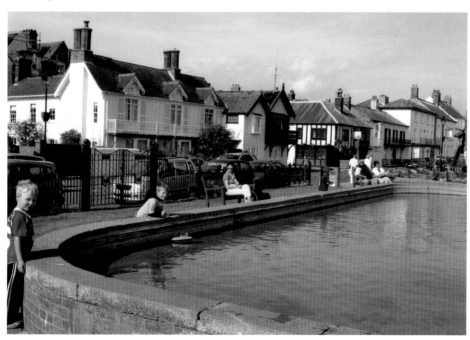

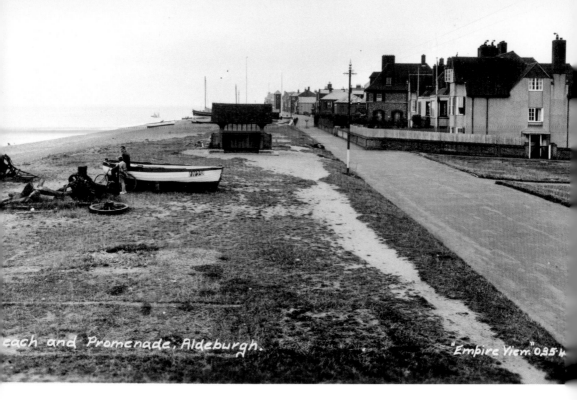

Beach and Promenade, Aldeburgh.   "Empire View" 035.4

Beach and Promenade

The Aldeburgh Pier and Improvement Company Limited was formed under the chairmanship of Colonel A. J. B. Thellusson. The company proposed to build a 561-foot pier between 1876 and 1878. It was begun off Crag Path near the Moot Hall but by the early 1880s it had been abandoned unfinished and was later demolished.

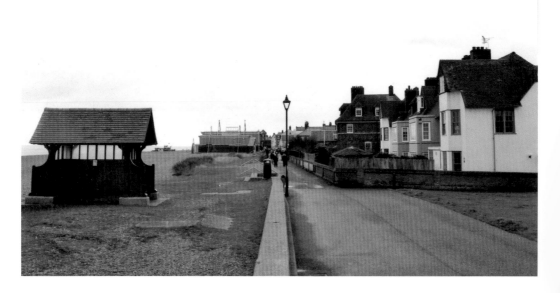

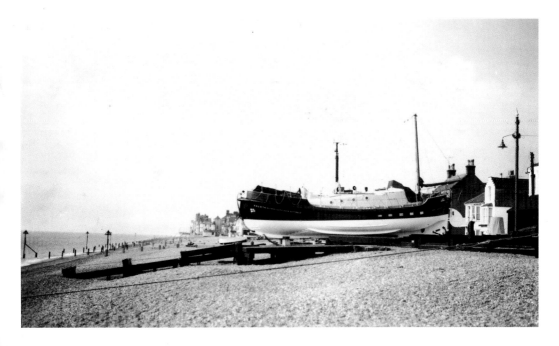

The *Alfred and Patience Gottwald* Lifeboat

This lifeboat was on station between 1959 and 1979. The sea off Aldeburgh is treacherous with sandbanks and shoals and the fierce gales that can blow up. In a long and glorious tradition the Aldeburgh lifeboats have saved many lives, including taking part in the evacuation of Dunkirk in 1940. In 1899 they suffered their own tragedy when seven crew members were lost. They are now commemorated by a memorial in the churchyard. Today's lifeboat, the Mersey class *Freddie Cooper*, is housed in the modern Penza boathouse and launched by tractor, where once it was all willing hands to help the launch and bring the boat back up the shingle beach.

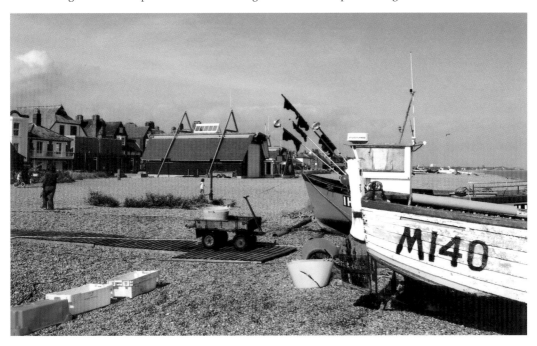

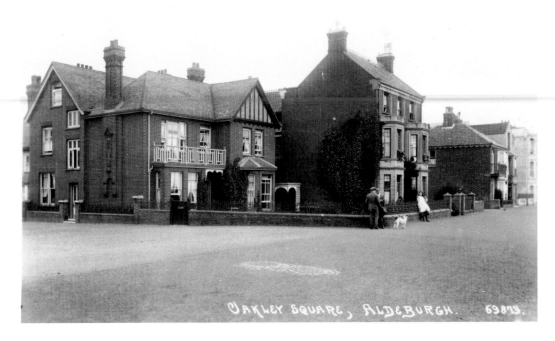

Oakley Square

A quiet square opposite the South Lookout tower, now almost inevitably a busy car park. In his book *In Quaint East Anglia*, published in 1899, West Carnie writes that Aldeburgh, 'if not a very advanced watering-place, has at least got some excellent hotels, good shops, and a splendid golf links to recommend it...At Aldeburgh you can be as energetic or a lazy as you like. You can do your thirty six holes on the links religiously every day, or you can lie for hours on the shingly beach and hunt for cornelian, agate or amber.'

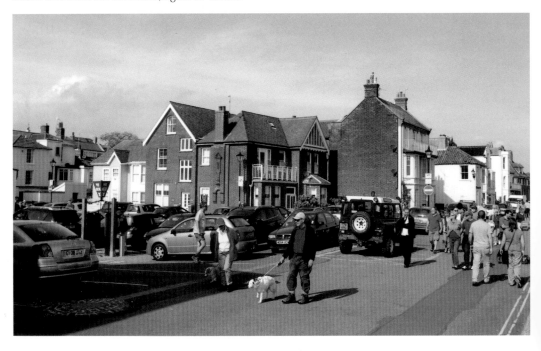

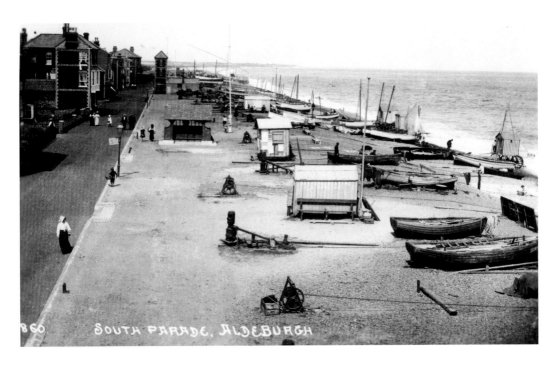

South Parade, Aldeburgh

A Typical Scene, *c.* 1937

Dorothy Thompson, writing in *Sophia's Son*, the biography of her father the Revd Henry Thompson (1841–1916), Vicar of Aldeburgh, gives a dramatic account of the battle against the sea: 'Great seas rolled in one after another in quick succession, each one reaching further up the beach until they broke over the top and water poured into the street. Windows were boarded up, boats and bathing machines were drawn up in front of the shop windows, and anxious seamen kept a look out on wind and tide.'

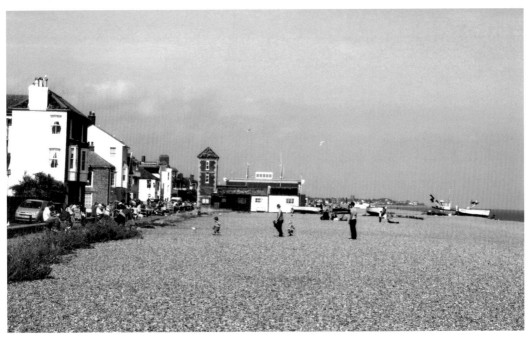

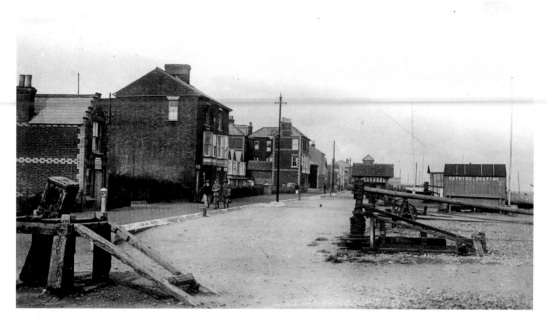

The Craig Path

It should be the Crag Path, but it is a lovely photograph, probably dating from the First World War to judge by the sad little message addressed to Miss May Elsworthy in Cardiff: 'Did not get your parcel. I suppose someone has enjoyed them. This is my billet.' During the First World War it was thought by the government that the most likely stretch of coast for an invasion was between Aldeburgh and Lowestoft.

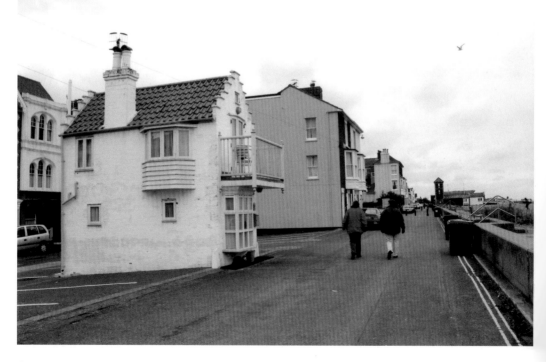

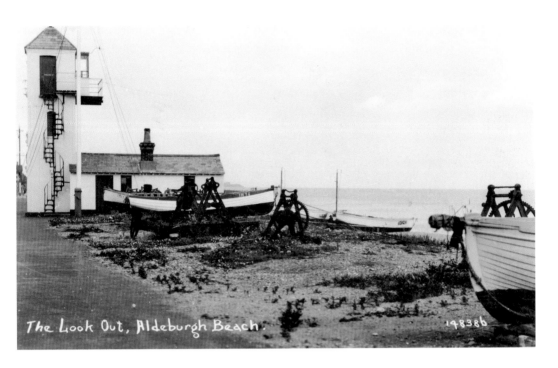

The Look Out, Aldeburgh Beach.

148386

The Lookout

This is the South Lookout. In 1851 Aldeburgh's population was 1,627. The railway opened in April 1896 and gave a great boost to the fishing industry, quickly moving the daily catches of sprats and herring inland, but shingle banks near the harbour gradually choked the industry. The railway continued to bring visitors to the town but it was about half a mile from the town and sea. The line was axed in 1966, but the Railway Inn survives on the Leiston Road.

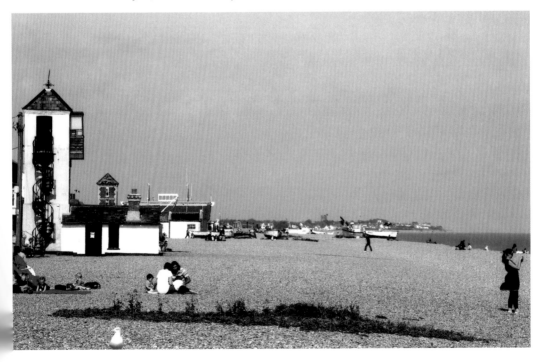

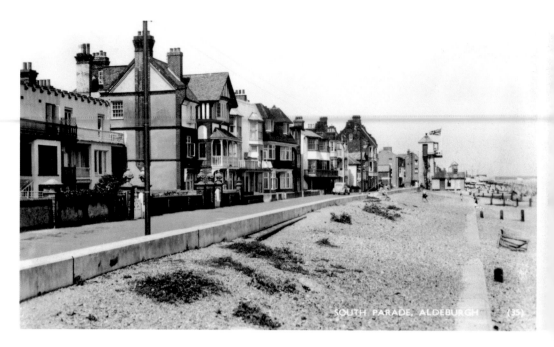

South Parade

A view that has changed very little in just over fifty years. The visitors lined up on the sea wall below are all enjoying Aldeburgh's famous fish and chips. There are notices about not feeding the gulls, but the gulls gather regardless. This defensive sea wall is not on the earlier photograph of Grosvenor Terrace.

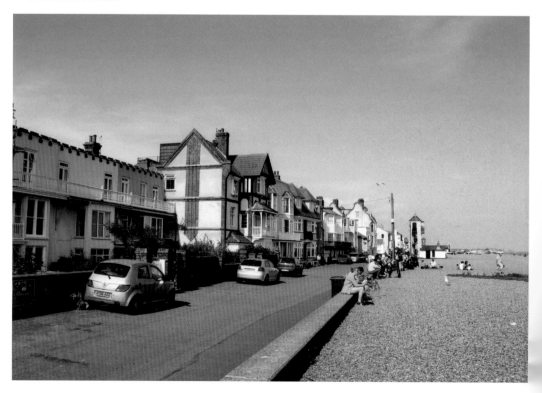

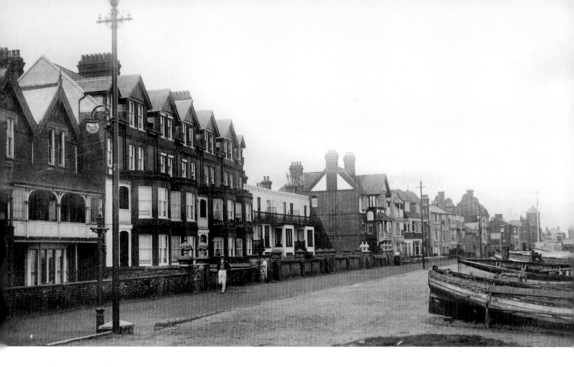

Grosvenor Terrace

A view dating from the First World War, with a fascinating message: 'Dear Sister, Just a line to let you know we arrived quite safe after a long journey of 800 miles. We only saw Philip for a few minutes as he had to go back in the trenches all night, but we hope to have a good word with him now.' Troops were billeted in the town and all along the coast, and Aldeburgh had a landing strip for the Royal Naval Air Service to combat the threat from the zeppelins.

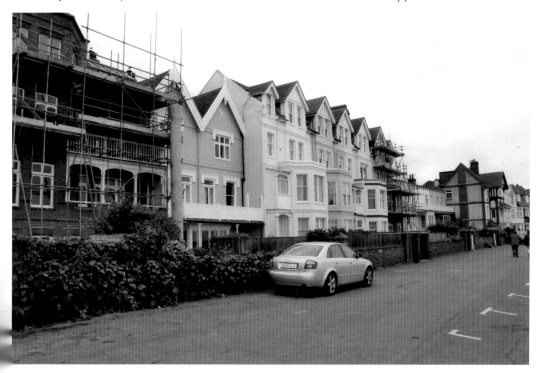

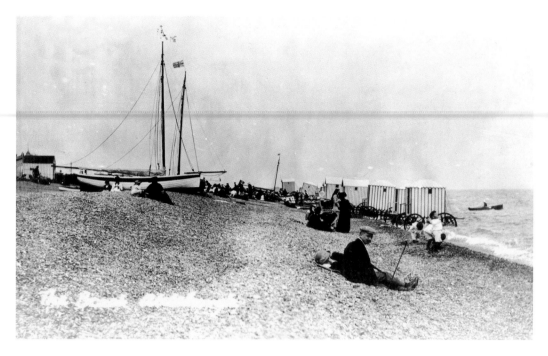

The Beach

According to the *Ward Lock & Co. Guide*, 1923/24, 'Restfulness and absence of excitement are characteristic of Aldeburgh. The visitor can read his book, or dream, with no fear of disturbance by beach minstrels or vendors.' It really hasn't changed much. There is space to escape the crowds. The shingle, which is difficult to walk across, is ridged to provide a comfortable place to recline in the sun. By the sea's edge the going is easier.

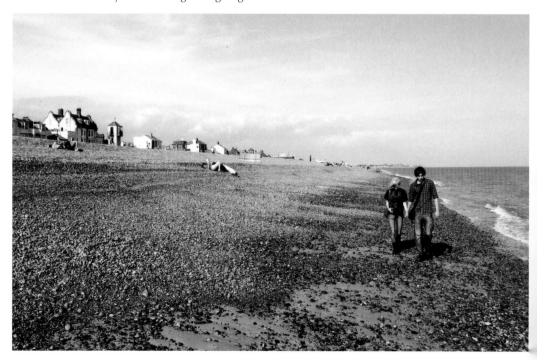

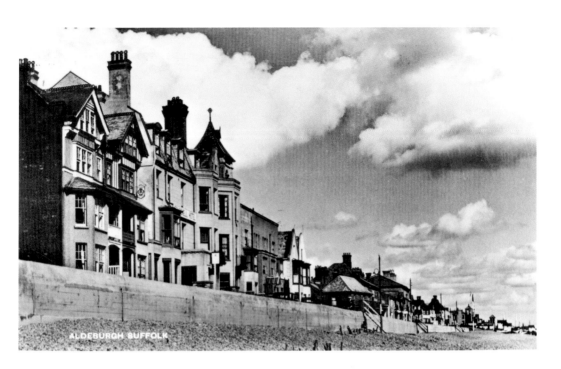

Brudenell Hotel

C. S. Ward wrote in the 1880s: 'the only block of houses near the sea that approximates to the ordinary type of seaside villa, is Brudenell Terrace'. The Brudenell Hotel, completely refurbished in 2010, was part of Brudenell Terrace, once owned by Newson Garrett. According to Leonard P. Thomson in *Inns of the Suffolk Coast*, the Brudenell name appears to come from Lady Augusta Brudenell-Bruce who married Frederick Wentworth, Lord of the Manor of Aldeburgh, in 1825. The first full licence was granted in 1868.

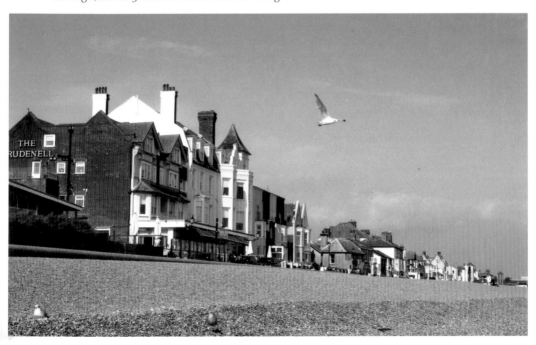

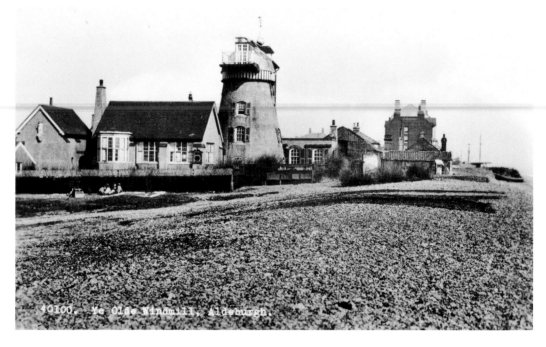

Ye Olde Windmill

This former tower mill on Fort Green was built in 1824 and converted into a residence in 1902. The southern end of Aldeburgh has always been vulnerable to the sea and the Fort Green area was overwhelmed in 1938 and again in 1949. The 1938 high tide swept away large parts of the promenade and swamped many of the seafront houses. Behind the windmill today there is an extensive area of visitor parking.

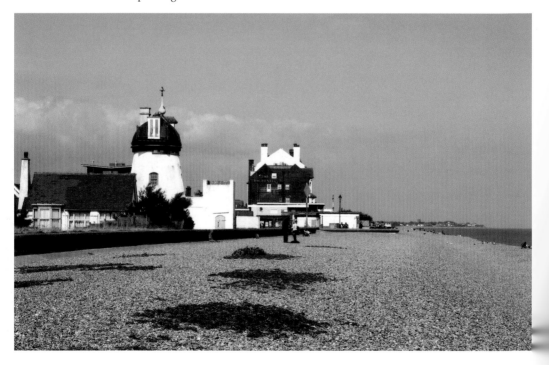

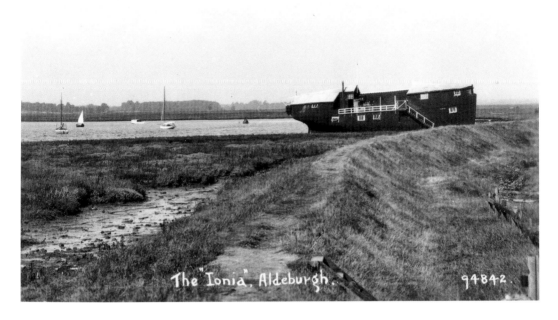

The "Ionia", Aldeburgh.   94842.

The *Ionia*, 1930

The *Ionia* was for many years a fascinating sight on the edge of the River Alde. The *Ionia* was a fishing smack that became stuck in the mud in 1872 and then converted into a houseboat. Old photographs of it remind me of a scene from a Charles Dickens story. By the middle of the twentieth century it was getting into a poor state, being eventually abandoned, and in 1974 it was burnt out.

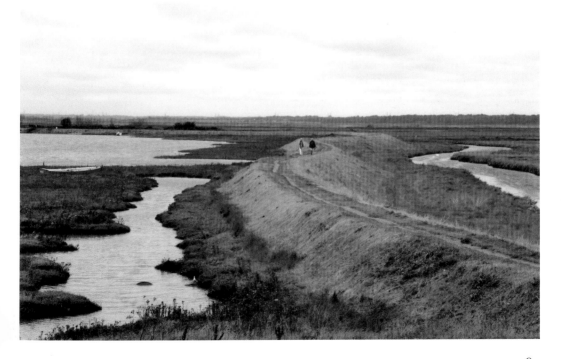

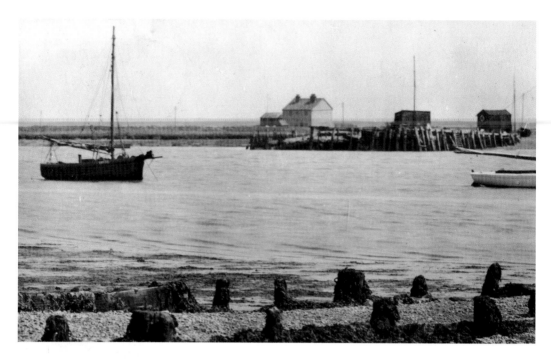

Slaughden Quay

Camden's *Britannia* (1586) describes Aldeburgh: ''tis a harbour very commodious for mariners and fishermen, by which means the place is populous, and is much favour'd by the Sea, which is a little unkind to other towns upon this coast.' In the seventeenth century there were three busy quays at Slaughden. There were warehouses and cottages, but the favours of the sea did not last. The effects of longshore drift moving the shingle along this stretch of coast exposed Slaughden to the force of the sea.

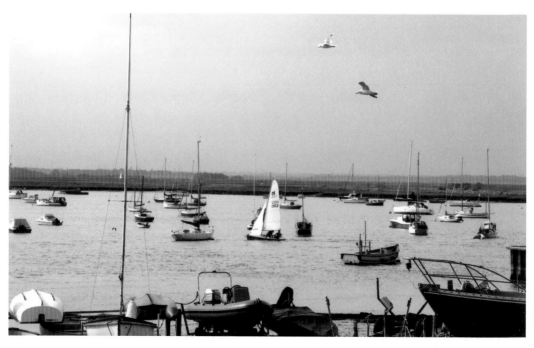

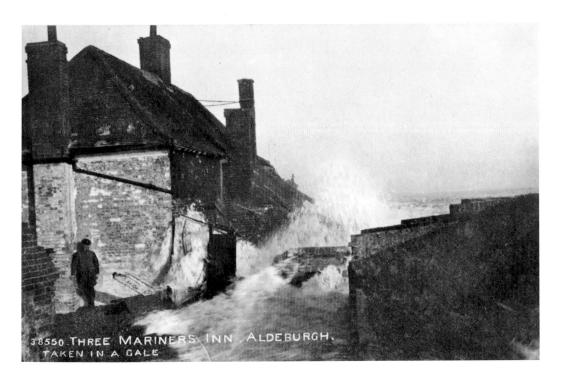

The Three Mariners

The Three Mariners was an ancient inn, reputedly the haunt of smugglers, standing among the other buildings along this now bare shingle ridge. It stood with its back to the sea, facing the Alde and the salt flats. There were times of high tides when the sea came in the back door and left by the front. Visitors were fascinated by its sign painted on a whale bone, a reminder of how Slaughden fishermen sailed to Icelandic waters. The inn was lost to the sea in 1910.

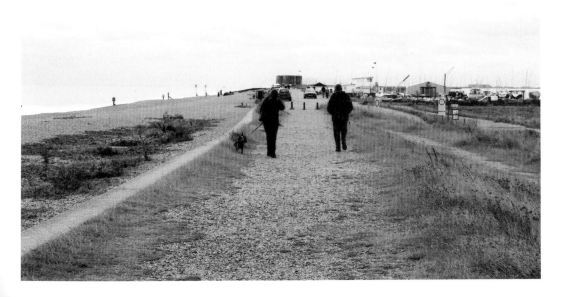

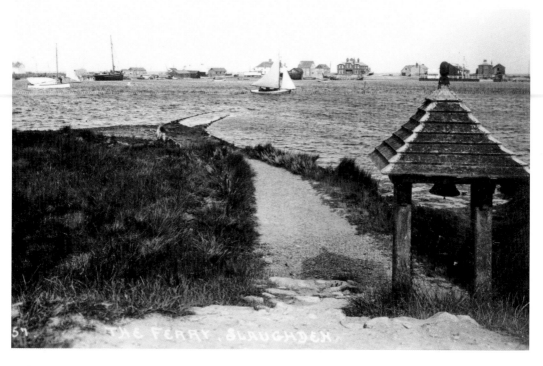

The Ferry

The ferry crossed the Alde from Slaughden to Iken. This photograph looks towards Slaughden showing the many buildings in the early years of the twentieth century. It also shows the wooden belfry where travellers wanting to cross to Slaughden and Aldeburgh summoned the boatman. There is still a ferry at Slaughden.

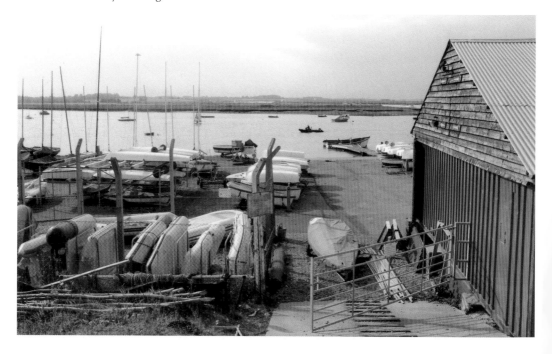

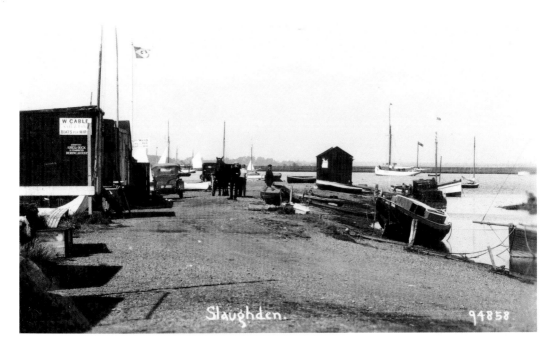

Slaughden. 94858

Slaughden

Today Slaughden has a flourishing yacht club and is a beautiful, if somewhat bleak, spot. It is popular with walkers and anglers. Beyond the Martello Tower is Orfordness, an extraordinary shingle bank separating the River Alde from the sea. This National Trust area is the largest shingle spit in Europe. This is an area of extensive sea defences, with groynes to try and stop the longshore drift, heavy boulders to break up the waves and extensive sea walls. Shingle is moved to strengthen the narrower parts of the spit, as any breach could bring extensive flooding around Aldeburgh.

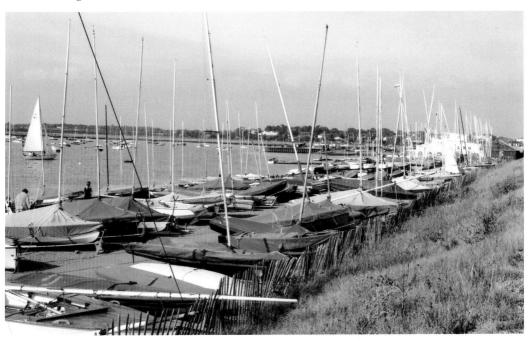

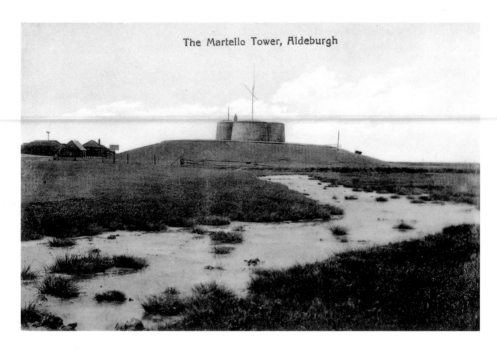

The Martello Tower, Aldeburgh

The Martello Tower, Slaughden, *c.* 1916

The most northerly of the chain of Martello Towers, which were built between 1808 and 1812 as a line of defence against invasion by Napoleonic forces. This tower is unusual as it is a quatrefoil design, like a four-leaf clover. The sea has claimed part of the moat but extensive sea defences in the 1950s now offer greater protection. In 1931 the tower was sold by the Ministry of Defence. It was privately owned and in a poor state of repair until 1971, when it was acquired by the Landmark Trust. The Trust carried out extensive repairs to the tower and it now provides holiday accommodation.

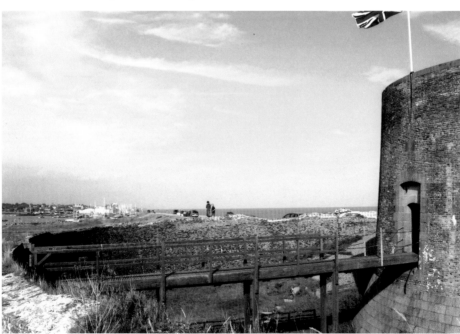

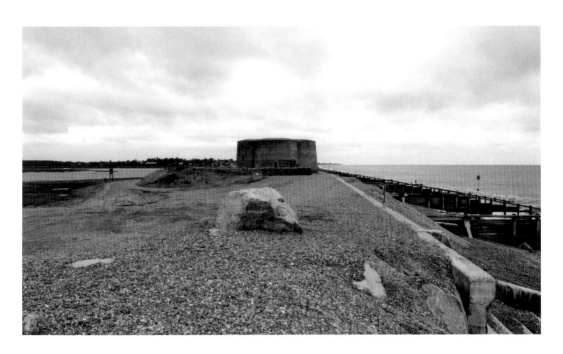

Sea Defences

It is possible to see how close the sea came to the Martello Tower and some of the defensive structures now in place. Throughout history this stretch of coastline has been at risk of invasion on several occasions, firstly by the Spanish and then by the French, which threat resulted in the construction of these towers. In the last century it was thought the Germans might invade along here. From 1913 the government has had a military bases here, firstly in the form of the central Flying School and later for atomic bomb testing and high-security American radar work. The biggest threat, however, remains – that 'best of friends, worst of enemies' – the sea. A breach of this spit could be catastrophic.

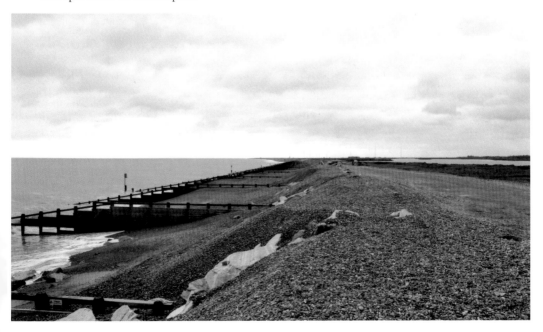

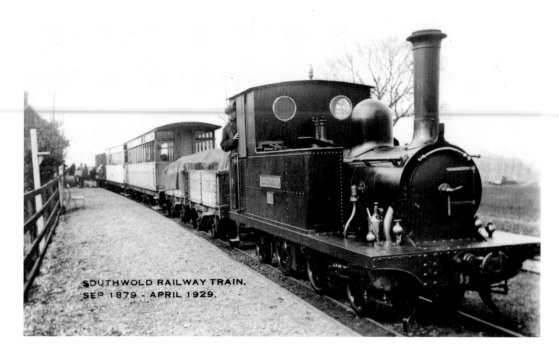

SOUTHWOLD RAILWAY TRAIN.
SEP 1879 - APRIL 1929.

Time Changes Everything

There is a plaque at the station site to mark the fiftieth anniversary of the closure of this quaint little railway. One can imagine enthusiasts running such a line today, had it survived. Instead much of the old track forms a cycleway. Some of the cyclists may be going as quickly as the little trains did, heading for that town by the sea, which waits like a favourite elderly aunt with everything neat and tidy, tea in a china cup and saucer, cucumber sandwiches and fancies for a treat. Relax and enjoy, it's Southwold.

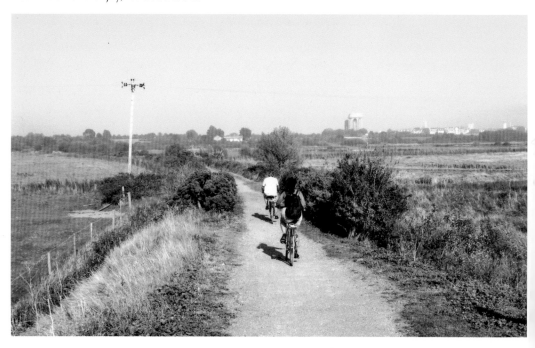